EDUCATION IN A MULTICULTURAL SOCIETY

Fred Rodriguez

UNIVERSITY
PRESS OF
AMERICA

LANHAM • NEW YORK • LONDON

Library of Congress Cataloging in Publication Data

Rodriguez, Fred.
Education in a multicultural society.

Bibliography: p.
1. Intercultural education–United States. I. Title.
LC1099.R63   1983   375'.0084   82–23755
ISBN 0–8191–2977–1
ISBN 0–8191–2978–X (pbk.)

DEDICATED TO :

Mary, Nathan and Jessica

iii

Table of Contents

EDUCATION IN A MULTICULTURAL SOCIETY

by

FRED RODRIGUEZ, ED.D.

Assistant Professor of Curriculum and Instruction
University of Kansas
Lawrence, Kansas

PREFACE

The 1960's and 1970's brought a new and dynamic challenge to American education. Members of groups whose histories and cultures had been omitted from or distorted within the mainstream curriculum began to request, sometimes demand, valid curricular inclusion. First Blacks, then Hispanics, Native Americans and Asian Americans called for reform. Then came the New Pluralism, with America's White ethnic groups appealing for the educational inclusion of their stories. Cutting across all racial, ethnic and mainstream American groups were women, and the handicapped, who rightfully pointed out both how their contributions had been omitted from curricula and how educational materials had become mired by the pervasive use of biased language. The time for change had come.

This book has been designed to guide you through the understanding and the development of your personal role in incorporating a multicultural perspective within your subject area and teaching style. You will not find any easy answers or prepared lessons here; so don't look for them. What you will find are some readings and exercises that hopefully will help you in guiding your thoughts and directing your planning.

The primary purpose of this book, "Education in a Multicultural Society," is two-fold: first, to heighten your awareness and sensitivity to the concept of multicultural education, and second, to provide you some suggestions and direction in the process of integrating this concept into your future curriculum designs and teaching philosophy.

On the following pages, the need for a multicultural concept is explained, its urgency and timelessness are stressed and some procedures are outlined. It's intent, however, is only to provide direction and suggestions. As a prospective classroom teacher, there is a responsibility to provide all of our students with the most meaningful educational experience we can. The multicultural concept is, at the very least, worth examining and thinking about in the formulation of our philosophy and attitudes that we will take with us in our classrooms. The contributions you make can only lead to an improved school situation and an increasingly mature multicultural perspective for you, your colleagues and for all of your future students.

America's Children -Alike- Yet, Different

Section 1:

What Do We Mean ....

Multicultural Education ?

Introduction
The rationale for incorporating a multicultural perspective within all schools comes from many sources. Teachers and their professional organizations, parent groups, colleges and universities, as well as public organizations, accreditation agencies and foundations have all expressed the view that all Americans need to better understand, respect, appreciate and accept the diversity that exists in our society.

This section provides insights into the concept of multicultural education. Simply, what do we mean by multicultural education? Why is it needed in today's schools? Who does it involve? And, a look at common reactions to those opposed to a multicultural perspective.

Section I is composed of some readings, position statements, rationales, policies and exercises designed to: 1) Provide a base knowledge for you, and 2) to begin to focus on your role and your response as a prospective classroom teacher, to a multicultural concept in education today and in the future.

What do we Mean?

The answer to this question has been and continues to be debated by many scholars in education. Is it a separate program, a unique course, or a particular curriculum to be added to the other school offerings available to students? Or is it a process, a philosophical orientation, an instructional theory for the delivery of quality education.

Multicultural education has developed from a number of educational concepts that have fluctuated in popularity during the past 30 years, including cross-cultural education, intercultural education, human relations, ethnic studies, and multiethnic studies. Terms serve as ground rules for perceiving and understanding educational concepts. Terms may have more than one meaning and thus may convey varying perceptions to different people. Multicultural education is no different. This type of variation frequently results in education programs that are weakly conceptualized, poorly designed and misinterpreted. Multicultural education fits into this dilemma. There are problems with consensus definitions, but it is essential for each of us to determine his/her own understandng of the concept. Perhaps, if we address the concept from what it is not, then maybe we may gain a clearer understanding of what it is.

What it is Not

Multicultural education is not a course or subject.

Multicultural education is not a unit on society's problems.

Multicultural education is not a system for teaching social studies.

Multicultural education is not aimed at training teachers to work exclusively with ethnic minority students.

Multicultural education is not solely intended for minority student populations or the geographic setting of the schools.

Multicultural education is not a program.

Then....

What IS Multicultural Education?

Multicultural education is education which values cultural pluralism. To endorse cultural pluralism is to endorse the principle that there is no one model American.

Multicultural education recognizes cultural diversity as a fact of life in American society, and it affirms that this cultural diversity is a valuable resource that should be preserved and extended.

Multicultural education rejects the view that schools should seek to melt away cultural differences and the view that schools should merely tolerate cultural pluralism.

Multicultural education recgnizes that no group lives in a vacuum - that each group exists as part of an interrelated whole.

Multicultural Education

and

Teacher Education

American Association of Colleges for Teacher Education

(AACTE)

Multicultural education programs for teachers are more than "special courses" or "special learning experiences" grafted onto the standard program.

Colleges and Universities engaged in the preparation of teachers have a central role in the positive development of our culturally pluralistic society. If cultural pluralism is to become an integral part of the educational process, teachers and personnel must be prepared in an environment where the commitment to multicultural education is evident.

The commitment to cultural pluralism must permeate all areas of the educational experience provided for prospective teachers.

Adapted from "No One Model American," Journal of Teacher Education, Vol. 24, No. 4 (Winter 1973), p. 264. Reprinted by permission.

Accreditation Standards

NCATE

National accreditation of colleges and university programs for the preparation of all teachers and other professional school personnel at the elementary and secondary levels is the responsibility of the National Council for the Accreditation of Teacher Education (NCATE).

In the NCATE standards for the Accreditation of Teacher Education, which became effective January 1, 1979, Multicultural Education is explicitly addressed.

Provisions for Multicultural Education must be evident

in undergraduate and graduate programs in order to

receive full accreditation.

NCATE, 1979, pps. 3-19

NCATE offers the following definition of multicultural education in the preamble of its standards:

Multicultural education is preparation for the social, political, and economic realities that individuals experience in culturally diverse and complex human encounters. These realities have both national and international dimensions. This preparation provides a process by which an individual develops competencies for perceiving, believing, evaluating, and behaving in differential cultural settings.

NCATE, 1979, pp. 3-19

5

North Central Accreditation

Education for Pluralism

Today it is widely recognized that our schools no longer can seek to prepare young American for a single-model, monolithic culture, for that is not the nation our young people are to inherit. To the contrary, the American culture that will fall into their hands is composed of innumerable variegated strands contributed by many different races, many different ethnic groups. The need for young people to understand, to appreciate, to respect the great human diversity of our country--to accept the fact that no one color, no one sex, no one tradition, no one heritage can lay exclusive claim to either the nation's history or its future-is exigent. Thus every school has the obligation to make education for pluralism a fundamental theme running throughout its entire program so that its graduates will be prepared to move forward with confidence and eagerness into a multivariant America, indeed, into that global cillage which the old has become.

North Central Guidelines, 1980

As of 1978, thirty-four (34) states address multicultural education in guidelines, regulations, legislation/policies.

AACTE, 1978

Education should be the process of helping everyone to discover his/her uniqueness. To teach her/him how to develop that uniqueness, and then how to share it, because that is the only reason for having anything.

Leo   Buscaglia

TURNABOUT IS FAIR PLAY . . .
THE STUDENTS' TURN

Fred Rodriguez

"A good teacher is primarily a unique personality. If good
teachers are unique individuals, we can predict from the start
that the attempts to find common uniqueness would be unlikely to
get results. . . . A good teacher is first and foremost a person
and this fact is the most important and determining thing about
him/her." (1) While many rhetorically concur with Combs, the
traditional pattern of undergraduate teacher training does little
to foster personal growth. Content mastery is viewed as of
primary importance.

For many years, educators have attempted to study and understand what makes good teachers. There are some things that we
know about teaching success and teaching competence.

What Research Indicates

There appears only a slight relationship between intelligence and success as a teacher. This is not to suggest that
teachers do not need to be intelligent. Rather, those who teach
are usually selected on the basis of intelligence, and within a
range of scores characteristic of teachers, differences in intelligence have not been shown to be crucial as it relates to competence.

A common misconception is that knowledge and subject matter
per se are major factors in teaching success. Except for oc-
casional studies of mathematics and physical science, research
findings report little such relationship. The relationship of
socioeconomic status to criteria of effectiveness is low. Research suggests that those from higher economic categories have
greater possibilities or success in any human endeavor than those
from lower groups for reasons that are not directoly related to
teacher education. Despite prejudice to the contrary, there is
no eveidence that marital status or sex of the teacher in any way
reflects effectiveness. Attitude toward teachers and teaching
seems to bear a small but positive relationship to teaching
effectiveness when it is measured against student gain in a
classroom.(2)

Now if these generalizations reflect something about what we
already know, then where should we turn our attention to for
direction in teacher education?

With all the millions of dollars and millions of hours of
work that have gone into understanding what effectiveness in

teaching is, there are really only four areas of the effectiveness dimension of teaching which are validated over and over
again as contributing to teaching effectiveness. These four
dimensions are:

1. That effective teachers are effective because they view
   teaching primarily as a human process involving human
   relationships and human beings. On the effectiveness
   continuum, the area of healthy, involving relationships
   seems to be something which mark every effective teacher.
2. That good teachers have a positive view of themeselves
   and of others.
3. That effective teachers are well informed.
4. That effective teachers are able to communicate what
   they know in a manner that makes sense to others.(2)

All very commonplace kinds of findings, for which we have
spent millions of hours and hundreds of millions of dollars. But
if these are the areas that seem to make a difference, obviously
our present practices in the training of teachers are, in my
opinion, not totally relevant to meeting those needs. So, where
should we turn our attention for direction in teacher education?

Often we fail to take advantage of the obvious resources
available to us. With this in mind, I thought it would be of
benefit to "hear" from the people who are the recipients of our
teachers. Thus, it is now the students' turn.

The Lawrence Study

"In your opinion, what are the characteristics of a good
teacher?"

This question was given to approximately 200 high school
students (grades 10-12) from Lawrence, Kansas, in the Spring of
1980. The same question was given to my class of students planning or thinking about entering the teaching profession (Introduction to Teaching). The responses from the two groups of students
are worthy of comparison and reflection in regard to our teacher
education programs. In their response to the question, our
prospective teachers listed several important qualities and
characteristics a good teacher should possess:
"One who can manage a classroom well"
"One who has patience"
"A person who knows their content and subject area well"
"A person wo can handle discipline"
"Ability to answer questions"
"One who can explain problems clearly"

8

"One who is fair"
"Someone who can motivate and show enthusiasm"
"A good sense of humor"
"Someone who cares"

These responses are indeed important qualities and characteristics, which we can all agree are necessary for good teachers to possess. However, in comparing their responses with the thoughts and opinions of the high school students, a very different "focus" was overwhelmingly stressed.

"Someone who understands me"
"Someone who can relate to me"
"Someone who can be a friend"
"Someone who treats me as an individual"
"Being a friend, instead of a teacher"
"Someone who talks with you, not at you"
"Someone who treats his/her students as individuals and gets to know each one personally; not as just some kid out of 2nd hour."

The message seems to come out loud and clear: "give us teachers who can relate to us, understand us, and someone who can be a friend to us." Turnabout is indeed fair play, and these students took a turn that does warrant attention to the product we are sending to them.

We in teacher education place a great deal of emphasis upon the students learning and understanding their subject area well, which is extrememly important and essential. We spend a great portion of time discussing and emphasizing the importance of using a diversity of teaching styles and techniques, and the need to always update ourselves. Also, we spend a great deal of time equipping our teacher candidate with the "tricks of the trade" that hopefully prepare them to better handle the unexpected surprises that come with the job. However, theories concerning classroom management, techniques for handling classroom problems, and "knowledge" of subject matter, does little good if our teacher candidates enter the classrooms of tomorrow and suddenly discover their inability to "get those things across."

As I have alluded to, the academic preparation we provide in the training of teachers seems irrelevant to the basic characteristics teacher candidates need. What are the implications?

Implications for Effectiveness

If it is true that good teachers are good because they view teaching primarily as a human process involving human relation-

9

ships and meaning, this might imply that we should spend at least as much time exposing and sensitizing teacher candidates to the subtle complexities of personality structure as we do to introducing them to the structure of knowledge itself.

If it is true that teachers should have a positive view of themselves and others, this might suggest that we provide more opportunity for teacher candidates to acquire more positive self--other perceptions. Self-concept research tells us that how one feels about hemself/herself is learned. If it is learned, it is teachable. May we should begin teaching that.

If it is true that good teachers are well-informed, then it is true that we must neither negate nor relax our efforts to provide them with as rich an intellectual background as possible. Teachers are usually knowledgeable people, and knowing and knowledge is the aspect of preparation with which teacher education has traditionally been most successful. Nonetheless, teachers rarely fail because of lack of knowledge. They fail more often because they are unable to communicate what they know so that it makes a difference in the lives of their students.

If it is true that good teachers are able to communicate what they know in a manner that makes sense to their students, then we must assist our teacher candidates through example and appropriate experiences that will be the most effective.

Our students "think" they know what today's students want in a teacher, but they really do not. Too often, many of our young teachers become confused, frustrated, and disillusioned by their sudden discovery of what today's classrooms and the students in them are like. Unless we in teacher education can provide some method for prospective teachers to have this direct personal contact with today's student beforehand, we will continue to have students entering the teaching profession with a very limited amount of contact and understanding of today's student.

The perception of those high school students was extremely enlightening for me. Their honest and open remarks have only reinforced my belief that the teaching profession and the ability to TEACH must start from a solid foundation--a foundation which is based on the quality and skill to express a humanness to others. There is no greater need for this quality than in ALL of our classrooms today and tomorrow.

Multicultural Education

and the

"BASICS"

The "back to the basics" movement continues to be the education media event of our time. But what is meant by "back to the
basics"? Might multicultural education be one of those "basics"
needed in our system of education?

The "back to the basics" slogan suggests several messages: (1)
There is a well-defined set of objectives in existence for well-
understood reasons; (2) There is a well-defined set of objectives
relative to each discipline; and (3) At some point in our educational
past, we were teaching these basics in a manner that deserves to be
revived now.[1]

In fact, on all three accounts, the contrary is true. Far
from the movement having well-defined reasons for existence, it
appears many advocates of the movement are on its "bandwagon" for
reasons other than in the interest of education.

The March 1977 issue of Phi Delta Kappan is devoted entirely
to the examination of this movement. In one article, Ben Brodinsky
asserts that his search for the causes of the movement found such
factors as : "nostalgia in the '70's, the public's whetted appetite
for accountability, the nation's periodic swing to conservatism;
the high divorce rate and the disintegration of the family, leading
to demands that the schools provide the discipline which the home
no longer can; the excess of permissiveness; and a bundle of the
causes in which Dr. Spock, T.V., and creeping socialism are all
crammed into one bag."[2]

Whatever the causes, I have difficulty in pinpointing just
what the movement is advocating. Objectives seems to range from
strict drill in the three R's to a more vague return of religious
and patriotic values to the curriculum and the elimination of such
"frills" as for example, multicultural education. So, while one
may or may not agree in spirit with the movement, absolute caution
must be take not to assume the "basics" of instruction and learning
are agreed upon, as well as, understood by all. What is basic to
one group of people is not necessarily basic to another.

Education in the United States historically has been Anglo-centric and dominated by the pervasive assimilationist forces in American society. A major goal of the common school was to help immigrants and ethnic group youths acquire the cultural characteristics and values of Anglo-Americans. The goals of the common school reflect legislation, which primarily is concerned with racial quotas, what has happened in the past continues to happen today. That is, minority and majority students are immersed in an edcational setting that is dominated by the Anglo-centric point of view. The experience continues to be one of viewing minorities as sterotypes, or entirely omitting minorities from the curriculum. For the majority student, an opportunity to acquire a better understanding and appreciation of others, as well as of themselves, is lost once again.

Granted, today we hear of a few schools in this country that are "active" and to some extent, successfully addressing some of these important educational concerns. However, one only needs to look a bit closer at the majority of those schools to determine the causes of such "active commitment": (1) The "threat" of a lawsuit lingers over their heads. (2) There is the recent "threat" of possibly losing their federal dollars if they are not providing equal educational opportunities for all students. (3) They have lost a battle in the courtoom and have been ordered to be "active." (4) They now are receiving some form of federal financial assistance to incorporate some "new" programs designed to benefit minority students. The list of reasons for such "committed" efforts can go on, but the point is this; educators and schools acrosss the country are involved "actively" in these educational concerns because of their reaction to some form of pressure from the community, legislation, or from the courts.

A case in point is the recent implementation of Title IX, which prohibits discrimination of the basis of sex in all educational institutions receiving federal financial assistance. The initial reaction to Title IX, was very similar to, if not the same as that to minority education programs, with many, REACTING to this legislation as something that "we have to do," rather than examining our past educational practices and admitting to the inequality of treatment we have provided for our students and ACTING upon Title IX as "the right thing to do." The same is true for multicultural education. We only need to hold back our pride and admit that we adopted an educaitonal philosophy and approach that has been slanted to the male, anglo-centric point of view. Then, we can begin to rectify this unfortunate situation, based upon our BELIEF, that this is the right thing to do for all students concerned. It is sad to think that in order to provide some degree of equality among our students in this country, we must be prodded by some form of legislation.

However, those schools which are so active- primarily represent the larger urban areas of this country. Consequently, there are countless schools that have not been affected by the pressure, legislation or court orders primarily because of the complacency of leaving things as they have been and the fact that "we don't have any minorities here" philosophy. The result, for the vast majority of schools in this country, regardless of their ethnic composition, is the continuance of the Anglo-centric, male-dominated approach. The endless cycle of frustration and resultant rejection by the educational system are experienced by the minority student.

But equally tragic, is the fact that the majority student is denied the opportunity of intellectual freedom and growth within the American system of education. We continue to graduate students from all levels who are "ignorant" of people who are different from themselves - ignorant, only because of a lack of knowledge and understanding. What can be more "basic" than to have the functional knowledge and understanding of all the people with whom we will live, love and share the rest of our lives?

WHAT MUST WE ALL DO?

CHANGE. A simplistic word for such a complex problem. This word has a tendency to frighten most of us. As educators, we have a great capacity to adopt and nestle with, what I call, our "self-patented" educational approach and philosophy. That is, once we get used to doing "our thing" in education a certain way, we adopt it and stick with it, until death do us part. Granted, we constantly are being bombarded by new and innovative ideas, but the majority of time, we tend to observe these movements as "fads" that we hope eventually will go away. So, why should I bother to change my "self-patented system? I'm not suggesting that what we were taught in the past and what we do now is all wrong, but if change comes so hard, how in the name of education will we ever move forward and continue to improve our skills? How tragic it is to see an educator who has been doing the same thing for the last 5,10, 15 or 20 years. It is very tragic, but painfully more common than we would like to admit. To change for the sake of change is wrong. To resist change because of some personal "hangups" is not only wrong, but detrimental to professional growth, and more importantly denies all students the opportunity to acquire the knowledge that is so critical for their own futures, as well as their present existence. Change is a "basic" educational must. We continually must update and seek alternatives that will best provide all students those necessary skills, experience and knowledge in our ever changing society.

BARRIERS TO CHANGE

The educational system does not support is members for being

13

different. Thus, feelings of personal inadequacy on the part of the
school administration and teachers result in low levels of personal
autonomy and a high level of hostility focused on out-groups which
pose real or perceived problems.[4] Change boils down to choices by
majority members between following a personal value system and
following the majority value system. Facilitating change begins
with the idea of personal responsibility for individual behavior.

Multicultural education is one of those needed changes that
will provide all students a more realistic life experience. But
somehow, the term multicultural education stirs in the minds of
some people the thought that this is an un-American and unnecessary
"frill." There always has been a deliberate and conscious effort
to find and treat differences as a basis of inequality. Once it was
called "survivial of the fittest." Today, it's the "haves" against
the "have nots." In a period when the technicans are able to bring
time, space, distance and peoples physically closer together, attitudes, beliefs, values and behaviors nevertheless are keeping
people far apart. Until all of us, from every strata in this society
can come to act and believe that to be different is still to be
equal, we cannot achieve the ultimate goal of a truly democratic
and pluralistic society. [5] Students must live the ideal that being
different doesn't matter.

HOW ? . . . AND THE REASONS WHY

If I were an American teacher or teacher-to-be today, the best
thing I could do to guarantee my own professional security and mo-
bility would be to make myself multicultural. The best thing that
I could do to give my students self-security would be to make them
able to function effectively in our multicultural society. For
example, if I were teaching minority students, I would do this in
such a way as not to harm their minority group membership, but
rather strengthen it, deepen it, and enrich it by adding to it as
much of the Anglo-American experience as I possibly could. If I
were teaching Anglo-American children, I would add to their good
fortune the additional sensitivity and perspective that comes from
knowing American minority cultures.

Multicultural education is not a favor for the ethnic minority
student; it is an obligation and opportunity for all of us to learn,
live and share with each other our unique identities and values.
What can be more "basic" in the educational process?

Education is more than reading, writing and arithmetic.
Education is preparation for life. Students need more than facts
and problem-solving skills; they need to know how to lead full and
useful lives in a complex world. In a nation made up of a variety
of races and nationalities, that means learning how to live and
work with people of different skin colors and cultural backgrounds.

A major goal for American public school education should be to
provide multiple experiences for all children. It should be as
desirable for children of the rich as for children of the poor to
know all kinds of people who live in this society. Thus, the opportunity to learn and work with peers from various cultural backgrounds must be provided from hour to hour and from day to day. If
this is what is meant by going "back to the basics," I'll jump on
your bandwagon!

References

1. Brodinsky, Ben, "Back to the Basics: The Movement and the
   Meaning." Phi Delta Kappan, March, 1977, p. 522.

2. Brodinsky, Ibid p. 523.

3. Banks, James A., "The Implications of Multicultural Education
   for Teacher Education," Pluralism and the American Teacher-
   Issues and Case Studies. Ethnic Heritage Center for Teacher
   Education, (AACTE), p.1

4. Oden, Chester W. Jr., "Desegragation and Mainstreaming: A
   Case of de'ya vu,"Mainstreaming and the Minority Child. 1976,
   p. 57.

5. Smith, William L., "Why Different Education for Different
   Groups?" Multicultural Education: Commitments, Issues, and
   Applications, ASCD, 1977, p.41.

The Teacher

and

Multicultural Education

Multicultural education is an encompassing concept. Consequently, developing an appropriate environment for it's incorporation has implications for every facet of the educational setting. First of all, the future of multicultural education depends on the ability of all who are involved in the educational system to assume the appropriate level of responsibility - state boards, local school boards, local school districts, administrators, and certainly, the classroom teachers. If and when this support system is in place, then multicultural education in our schools is imminent; because then, teachers like yourselves, will have the necessary support system to ensure successful implementation. Accordingly, with such support behind you, the degree to which multicultural education becomes a reality in our schools depends largely upon the attitudes and behaviors of the classroom teachers. The role and responsibility of the classroom teacher is vitally crucial to the future and the success of a multicultural perspective in our schools.

Your Attitude and Behavior

Teachers do play a significant role in the formation of children's attitudes. Research suggests that next to parents, they are[1] the most significant people in children's lives. Thus, the burden placed upon teachers is great. For example, children bring biases and prejudices to the classroom. Studies have found that they come to school with previously established negative attitudes about people who are different than themselves. When this happens, it becomes necessary for teachers to deal with these existing attitudes and to encourage the students to develop accurate and positive images of such people.[2,3,4] If this cannot be done, our entire educational system must share the responsibility for endorsing a monocultural view of society that is inconsistent with the past and present realities of life in the United States.[5]

16

Teachers, too, bring to the classroom biases and prejudices toward people who are different from themselves. These predispositions can influence the communication of accurate and objective information about diversity in the educational setting. In addition, it is highly likely, that many teachers lack factual information about cultural diversity, religious diversity and economic diversity. This is not surprising because teachers, too, are the products of their education and training. More often than not, the tendency is to teach the way we were taught.

Of equal importance is the teacher's commitment to the value, the worth and the dignity of every child in the classroom. The way in which the teacher acts out the way he/she feels will set the pattern for students.[6] Behavior is as important as attitude because it demonstrates the attitude. Therefore, the teacher's behavior will reflect the teacher's feeling about the student. A sensitivity to the multicultural concept and an acceptance of the viability of these diverse lifestyles are also necessary before information about them can be taught. It is therefore imperative for all teachers, through classroom instruction, to develop attitudes and behaviors conducive to living in a pluralistic society.

References:

1. Wilbur B. Brookover and Edsel L. Erickson, Society, Schools and Learning. (Boston: Allyn and Bacon, 1969).

2. Kenneth B. Clark, Prejudice and Your Child (Boston: Beacon Press, 1955).

3. Mary Ellen Goodman, Race Awareness in Young Children, (London: Collier-Macmillian, 1952).

4. Bruno Lasker, Racial Attitudes in Children (New York: New American Library, 1970).

5. William W. Joyce and James A. Banks, eds. Teaching the Language Arts to Culturally Different Children (Reading, Mass: Addison-Wesley, 1971).

6. Maxine Dunfee, Ethnic Modification of the Curriculum (Washington, D.C.: ASCD, 1969).

Your Thoughts....

How do you, as a prospective classroom teacher, feel about a multicultural perspective? How do you feel about what has been said up to this point? Remember your personal response to multicultural education does not require you to agree with everything that is said. All that I do ask, is that you <u>think</u> about it with me and formulate some ideas on your own.

Write down what you believe to be some of the more important statements, ideas, thoughts, etc., that you have read so far.

_____

_____

_____

_____

_____

_____

Why do you believe these to be so important?

_____

_____

On the other hand, are there any statement(s) or assumptions with which you do not agree? What are they?

_____

_____

Why don't you agree with it?

_____

_____

Defining Multicultural Education

For you to have a true participatory role in implementing a multicultural concept in your future school/subject area, you must develop your own concept of multicultural education. I want you to consider how a multicultural perspective will affect you, your school, your department, your students and most importantly your teaching!

I believe it is essential for each and every one of us to come up with his/her own definition for multicultural education, but I want to give you some guidance along the way. There are problems with consensus definitions so I will not attempt to provide one. However, I have collected some definitions written by students like yourselves, and offer them as a sample for you to consider.

"Multicultural education is the concept which promotes crosscultural understanding and acceptance and the celebration of differences."

"Multicultural education reaches beyond isolation and chauvinism recognizing the obligation of each human being to every other human being at the same time preserving the rightful self-interests of all."

"Multicultural education is a set of competencies needed to enhance an individual's effective and responsible participation in society's affairs."

"Multicultural education is attaining an increased awareness of the broad societal perspectives essential to an understanding of our society as it is today and will be tomorrow."

"Multicultural education is an educational concept which endorses cultural pluralism as a reality."

"Multicultural education is an educational approach which involves all schools, persons and disciplines which will provide all students with a more meaningful and relevant educational experience."

Your Personal Response

To Multicultural Education

Look over what you have read so far and the definitions of multicultural education provided. Now, plan and write your own definition in the space below. Your definition should be different from any suggested. It should reflect your unique multicultural perspective and your future educational responsibilities.

My Definition

_____

_____

_____

_____

_____

_____

_____

Now, answer this question. Think about it. Your answer is very important. DO YOU BELIEVE THAT YOU, AS ONE INDIVIDUAL, CAN CONTRIBUTE TO THE IMPLEMENTATION OF A MULTICULTURAL CONCEPT IN YOUR SCHOOL?

( ) YES   ( ) NO

How Would you Respond?

1. There just isn't enought time to add on all these new ideas and content..... Besides, people in the social studies area can handle it better.

_____ Agree   _____ Disagree

Why? _____

_____

_____

_____

2. I really don't plan on teaching in a school setting or a community with a large ethnic minority population.

_____ Agree   _____ Disagree   Why? _____

_____

_____

_____

_____

3. I'm not so concerned with my students knowing "multicultural stuff" but whether she/he can read and write. Let's stick to the 3 R's and forget all these "frills" in education.

_____ Agree   _____ Disagree   Why? _____

_____

_____

_____

4. Differences. Why make such a big deal about it? We're all Americans here. We don't need to identify ourselves with "ethnic groups." We're Americans.

_____ Agree   _____ Disagree   Why? _____

_____

_____

_____

5. Multicultural education will promote "separatism" of America, rather than "uniting" all of our citizens.

_____ Agree   _____ Disagree   Why? _____

_____

_____

_____

_____

6. America is a melting pot. Everyone has an equal chance. If you want to make it in this country, all you need is a little desire and initiative.

_____ Agree   _____ Disagree   Why? _____

_____

_____

_____

_____

7. Change. Why change the educational approach? I went through the system without a multicultural focus and I don't think I was limited by it.

_____ Agree   _____ Disagree   Why? _____

_____

_____

_____

What is a Pupil ?

A Child of God - Not a Tool of the State

Who is a Teacher ?

A Guide - Not a Guard

What is the Faculty ?

A Community of Scholars - Not a Union of Mechanics

Who is the Principal ?

A Master of Teachig - Not a Master of Teachers

What is Learning ?

A Journey - Not a Destination

What is Discovery ?

Questioning the Answers - Not Answering the Questions

What is the Process ?

Discovering Ideas - Not Covering Content

What is the Goal ?

Opened Minds - Not Closed Issues

What is the Test?

Being and Becoming - Not Remembering and Reviewing

What is the School ?

Whatever we choose to make it

Allan A. Glatthorn

Section 2 :

A Pluralistic Society?

Viewpoints and Values

<u>INTRODUCTION</u>

"The ethnic problem within the United States at some point
has to emerge simply because we were lied to, accepted the
lie, and there is no greater danger to a person who fools
themselves. We expect the opposition to fool us; but when
we fool ourselves we are in deep trouble. We consistently
have fallen for the old melting-pot concepts. But there
never was a melting pot; there is not now a melting pot;
there never will be a melting pot; and if there were, it
would be such a tasteless soup that we would have to go
back and start all over!"

-Bayard Rustin-

Section 2 is designed to examine three fundamental questions:

1. Do we want cultures that differ significantly from each
other or do we want cultures that differ in name and history
only?

2. Do we wnat schooling that accentuates awareness of cultural
differences or do we want schooling that minimizes them?

3. Do we want ethnicity to persist or do we want it to slip
away unobtrusively?

The melting pot, separatism and cultural pluralism . . . . .
. Where are we? More importantly, where are headed? This section will examine the three principal theories that are existent
today, and a scattering of exercises will assist you in determining your philosophy in regard to the melting pot, separatism and
cultural pluralism.

We all have viewpoints and values which we hold firmly onto,
which may make our acceptance and appreciating "other" perspectives difficult.

This section will help focus our direction and planning with
regard to one aspect of multicultural education, that is, ethnicity in the United States.

......searches for a new way to define what it means to be an
American. We embrace the American dream as culturally
pluralistic- a nation having a unity of spirit and ideal, but a
diversity of origin and expression, a nation not of atomic individuals, but of dynamic, interacting groups, each of which brings
forth its best to help build a just and equitable society, free
of isolation, segregation, and racism. We believe that people
who are secure in their past and joyful in their present cannot
but be hopeful in their future. We call this the "new
ethnicity."

-The Orchard Lake Center for Polish Studies
and Culture.

Melting Pot

Separatism

Cultural Pluralism

Where Are We?

ANALYSIS OF AMERICA'S ETHNIC COMPOSITION

The Melting Pot as a Solution

There are two differenct theories of the melting pot. One expects minority groups to lose their special background and heritage and become an Anglo-American white steeped in British traditions. The other expects minorities to mix with Anglo-Americans to create a new American. In both cases, minority group members will lose their ethnic background. The grandsons of Irish or Italian immigrants will be the same as the great-grandsons of English or Scotch immigrants.

There are many advantages to society in the melting pot idea. Everyone would speak the same language, share the same traditions, and agree about most basic values. Tensions arising out of ethnic or racial differences would be non-existent.

Yet there are disadvantages too. America has grown great and strong partly because of the continuing contributions of different peoples. Europeans, Africans, and Asians who have refused to "melt" continue to contribute to the richness and variety of our culture. If all ethnic groups were assimilated, this immense variety would be lost. Also, some believers in the melting pot idea believe that non-whites are inferior and should not be allowed to melt and share in the good things of American life. In so doing, anger and frustration grows among the excluded groups and the result is serious ethnic tensions and conflicts.

The melting pot has advantages and disadvantages for individuals as well as for society. In a society where everyone is alike, men are likely to be treated as individuals. Discrimination along ethnic lines is not likely to exist, but to escape discrimination by being like everyone else, a minority group member would have to give up his dearest customs, traditions, and language. He might have to give up something deep-rooted, say, the lovely Christmas customs of his ancestral land, for something essentially meaningless to him the commercial "Xmas" which so many Americans celebrate. If he tried to hide his background, he would have to give up not only his tradition, but his family and friends as well, and live in fear of discovery. For most non-whites, pretending they are something they are not or giving up special traditions is a waste of time. They find themselves discriminated against anyway because of their skin color.

Melting Pot

Separatism as a Solution

The other side of the melting pot coin is separatism, the idea that for a minority to survive it must live apart. In practice, an ethnic or minority group would live in a totally separate section in a city or a state. It would have its own stores, churches, and teach its own tongue as a second language in the neighborhood schools. It would try to preserve its own way of life as much as possible.

The most extreme advocates of this view insist that separatism be complete. Some black leaders, for example, have argued that certain states be set aside for Blacks so they can live completely apart from other Americans. Some claim that both societies benefit from separatism. Advocates of this argue that the United States would be better off because it would no longer have "unmeltable" groups in it to cause tensions or challenge values. Separatists feel that their group would no longer be the object of hate, discrimination, and physical violence. Living alone they could preserve their traditions without threat from anyone. Yet separatism has many disadvantages for both the nation and the separatists. If one group were to physically withdraw from the nation, others might follow, and the nation might fall apart. New countries carved out of the United States would squabble with each other over boundaries and control of rivers. Reduced contact between ethnic groups would increase the already high levels of stereotyping and suspicion. As most separatist groups are poor, they would find themselves hard-pressed for capital to build a new nation, and their economic problems would be severe.

Individual separatists might be willing to pay the price of economic hardship, possible conflict with other nations, or limited contact with other people's traditions. In their own land they would be rid of discrimination and persecution and be free to develop their own values and traditions.

Sepa ˙ratism

Cultural Pluralism as a Solution

An alternative to separatism and the melting pot was suggested by a sociologist names Horace Kallen in the early part of this century. Kallen saw that many immigrant groups, white ethnics, Jews, and Catholics were trying to preserve their rich heritages in the face of pressures to lose them. He suggested that America needed these and other people's contributions, that America could be a cultural democracy, a place where groups could retain their traditions, yet still participate freely in American life. He expected that all groups would have to adapt some of their customs and beliefs, but there would be none of the old melting pot assimilation. Rather, each would be a distinct tile in a mosaic, separate but still part of a larger pattern. He called this cultural pluralism.

These ideals helped many immigrants, especially Catholics and Jews, to defend their decisions to preserve their religious heritages and many of their customs. Today it is particularly important to those members of minority groups who reject separatism but who also reject the melting pot such as Blacks, Asians, Hispanics, American Indians and others.

These groups have begun to put heavy value on their own history, art, music and culture. "Black is beautiful," "Brown, Red, and Black Power," the creation of minority study programs at colleges and high schools are expressions of cultural pluralism. So are special clothes, hair styles, and speech, which along with celebrations and holidays are a way of creating a feeling of solidarity among groups.

Advantages and Disadvantages

Like the melting pot and separatist solutions, cultural pluralism has advantages and disadvantages for both society and the individual. As it fosters respect for others and values difference, cultural pluralism reduces discrimination and social conflicts. This is good for society but there are costs too. In a pluralist society, signs, schools, courts of law might have to be bilingual and bicultural. People might resent having to learn everyone else's customs and languages and, as a result, might begin to drift toward separatism with its threat to the nation's unity. Individuals would be under strains in a culturally pluralistic society. Where difference is valued and upheld by law people have to be extra accepting and open to new foods, habits, and life styles. Many people--minorities and majority groups alike--have difficulty when they are confronted with sharp differences, with what they see as threats to their way of life. Yet all people can be enriched by their neighbors' customs. People who have long been melted into American culture might rediscover their own customs and past. Minority group peoples would at last be free to enjoy the full promise of American life without having to give up their ancient heritage. Thus, a genuine pluralism would allow each group to keep its ethnic identity alive while enabling all Americans to enjoy the spice and variety that comes from a people representing a host of traditions.

Cultural Pluralism

America is a Tossed Salad

Ethnicity in the United States

1. What is an ethnic group?

   _____

   _____

   _____

   _____

2. What is an ethnic minority group?

   _____

   _____

   _____

3. Are all ethnic groups defined by the same factors? Explain. (Provide an example)

   _____

   _____

   _____

   _____

4. What value is there in maintaining ethnic group cohesion?

   _____

   _____

   _____

5. Why do some ethnic groups isolate themselves from the mainstream of American society?

   _____

   _____

   _____

   _____

DIFFERENT VIEWPOINTS ON AMERICA'S ETHNIC COMPOSITION

Directions: Each of the following items presents a particular view of the nature of American society with regard to its ethnic composition. Some clearly illustrate a belief in the melting pot while others represent a separatist point of view, and still others represent a middle ground between these two extremes, cultural pluralism. Under each item place an X on the continuum to indicate the perception of America's ethnic character as presented in the statement.

1. My parents decided never to teach us German. They hoped that thereby we would gain a generation in the process of becoming full Americans.

Melting Pot   Cultural Pluralism   Separatism

2. Our blood is as the flood of the Amazon, made up of a thousand noble currents all pouring into one. We are not a nation, so much as a world.

Melting Pot   Cultural Pluralism   Separatism

3. Outwardly I lived the life of the white man, yet all the while I kept in direct contact with tribal life. While I had learned all that I could of the white man's culture, I never forgot that of my people. I kept the language, tribal manners and usages, sang the songs and danced the dances.

Melting Pot   Cultural Pluralism   Separatism

4. That's right--I was ashamed of my name. Not only that, I was ashamed of being a Jew. There you have it.... Exit Abraham Isaac Arshawsky.... Enter Art Shaw! You see, of course, how simple this little transformation was. Presto, Chang-o! A new name, a new personality. As simple as that.

Melting Pot   Cultural Pluralism   Separatism

33

5. Indian children are taught "to be like a white man, and think like a white man." They completely lose their self-identity as Navajos....

Melting Pot   Cultural Pluralism   Separatism

6. There are plenty of Italians here, men who a few years ago had nothing and now have so much money that they could not count all their dollars in a week. The richest ones go away from the other Italians and live with the Americans.

Melting Pot   Cultural Pluralism   Separatism

7. There are many sections of the United States in which even the third generation of immigrants does not speak English.

Melting Pot   Cultural Pluralism   Separatism

8. What I should like to do is come to a better and more profound knowledge of who I am, from where my community came, and where my son and daughter, and their children's children, might wish to head in the future: I want to have a history.

Melting Pot   Cultural Pluralism   Separatism

9. Hey! Why all the attention on the "minorities"? Why not emphasize Irish-Americans, German-Americans, Swedish-Americans?

Melting Pot   Cultural Pluralism   Separatism

34

10. It makes no difference to me whether my students are black, white or brown. They are <u>students</u> and I treat them all the same. After, all, we are all human beings. Why can't we forget about color entirely and just treat each other like human beings.

Melting Pot   Cultural Pluralism   Separatism

11. I'm not respected as a teacher. I'm referred to as, our minority teacher.

Melting Pot   Cultural Pluralism   Separatism

12. Michael, my boy, you are beginning to understand our American ways, and the sooner you drop your Serbian notions, the sooner you will become an American.

Melting Pot   Cultural Pluralism   Separatism

13. There is nothing wrong with the Black race except that the majority of them will not accept the standards, rules, and ways given to them by the Whites, and I do believe these rules are equal and fair for both Black and White.

Melting Pot   Cultural Pluralism   Separatism

14. Bilingual/Bicultural Education is detrimental to the progress a student makes. Teach them English as quickly as possible. That's what they will need in order to succeed in American society.

Melting Pot   Cultural Pluralism   Separatism

15. I'm not a minority, I'm Japanese.

_____

Melting Pot   Cultural Pluralism   Separatism

16. More and more, I think in family terms, less ambitiously, on
    a less than national scale. The differences implicit in
    being Slovak, and Catholic, and lower-middle class seem more
    and more important to me.

_____

Melting Pot   Cultural Pluralism   Separatism

17. Americans who do not speak English should learn it or go
    back where they came from.

_____

Melting Pot   Cultural Pluralism   Separatism

18. We demand that...Spanish be the first language and the
    textbooks be rewritten to emphasize the heritage and the
    contributions of the Hispanics.

_____

Melting Pot   Cultural Pluralism   Separatism

19. The Ohio Board of Education ruled that two Amish secondary
    schools,... would have to measure up to state standards or
    close. The Amish schools, the board said, have no graded
    courses in geography, American history, natural sciences,
    government, and other required subjects. Some teachers, the
    board added, have no more than an eighth-grade education.

_____

Melting Pot   Cultural Pluralism   Separatism

20. The Amish want to keep to themselves--a separate people.
    They are tied together by their religion and its values, by
    kinship (most of them are related), and by customs that make
    them seem different from everyone else.

    _____

    Melting Pot   Cultural Pluralism   Separatism

21. Why can't we learn to appreciate, accept and respect 'dif-
    ferences' in this country? To merely "tolerate" people
    doesn't make it a better place to live.

    _____

    Melting Pot   Cultural Pluralism   Separatism

AN EXPERIENCE IN CHOICE, DISCRIMINATION, PREJUDICE, AND VALUES

Purpose: To provide the participant with an experience that will
sensitize him/her to the inter-working of choice,
discrimination, prejudice, and values within him/
herself as well as others.

Introductions: Your are a member of a team of teachers who must
establish a fourth grade, 15 student class roster from
the attached list and descriptions of candidates. The
only special criteria to be used in completing this
task are the following:

1. Each participant is to first independently list his/her
personal choices of the 15 students to be included by
name;

2. The 15 students selected should be rank-ordered in the
list from first to last choice;

3. Selections and rejections should be made thoughtfully,
with the participant prepared to defend his/her choices
by explanatory rationale;

4. You will have 30 minutes to complete the above three
steps;

5. Following the completion of the first three steps, each
participant will share his/her choices and reasons with
the other members;

6. The team's collective task will be to establish
consensus regarding which of the 22 students will be
included, their rank-order, and the explanatory rationale to final choices and rankings;

7. The team will have 45 minutes to accomplish steps 5 and
6 above.

Adapted from TEACHING IN A MULTICULTURAL/PLURALISTIC SOCIETY, by
Amos, Jones, Williams & Brooks, Wright State University, Summer
1980. Reprinted by permission.

Candidates for Class Roster

LYNDA:
Lynda is a truly gifted youngster with an I.Q. of 140. She knows it and flaunts it. She is good in all academic subjects and demands a lot of extra preparation time from her teachers. Her grades are excellent.

JUDY:
Judy is a "sweet young lady." She is always very polite and mannerly. Her classmates see her as the "teacher's pet." Judy has generally good grades overall and is especially good in Language Arts. She tends to "lord" strengths and assets over other children.

BILLY:
Billy is a very clumsy boy who trips over everything: his own feet, cracks in the sidewalk, etc. His performance in all subjects is mediocre. He is somewhat of a management problem because, although not disruptive, he tends to be aggravating and provocative to others.

CHARLES:
Charles is the class tattle-tale. He informs on who is talking when the teacher leaves the room, on who was fighting at lunchtime, in fact, on anyone about anything. His grades are fair; he is, however, good in art and music. Charles constantly seeks adult approval.

HENRY:
Henry is generally rejected by his peers. He is noticeably poorer than his classmates and seems to be always dirty. His grades overall are about average and he is especially good in art and physical education. He presents no major behavior management problem, but is occasionally known to be a whinner.

PETER:
Peter has very effeminate mannerisms, such as girlish walk and giggle. While he is good in science and reading, his grades are generally low average. He presents no special classroom management problem other than the other students' tendency of teasing him by calling his "sissy."

NANCY:
Nancy is best described as "scatterbrain" or a permanent "lunchbreak." She does things such as attempting math and reading seatwork simultaneously, and winds up doing neither accurately or completely. Her grades are generally poor to

39

fair, but she is good in art. She requires constant reminders and verbal instruction from teachers.

SUSAN: Susan is a very mature youngster who presents no problems to her teachers of any kind. She does her work, minds her own business, shows socially well-adjusted behavior, and is a favorite with her classmates. She is good in all subjects and has excellent grades. She is often used by her teachers as a very helpful peer-tutor to her slower classmates.

THEORDORE: Theodore, "Teddy" to his friends and "Teddy-Bear" to his girlfriends, is a boy whose greatest ambition is to become a "pimp" as soon as he's old enough. Rumor has it that he is already recruiting his "stable" from the girls in the fourth grade. "Teddy" presents no consistent or specific classroom management problems, but he tends to be sneaky and bears close watching. His grades are generally good and especially so in math, science, and social studies.

MICHAEL: Michael is a braggart who exaggerates all re-told personal experiences to fantastic proportions. His "tale-spinning" is somewhat disruptive to the class and he demands a great deal of his teachers' attention. While his grades are generally average, he is good in art and music.

GRACE: Grace is a very bossy and talkative girl who is always ordering her classmates around. Her classmates get very angered by her behavior and she has few friends as a result. While being generally well-behaved, she often presents classroom management problems engaging in power struggles with teachers as instruction giving rivals. Her grades are generally good and she is especially good in language arts.

NEIL: Neil is a smart aleck, sassy youngster. He can be described as a "motor-mouth" who is always quick with flip "put-down." There is nobody he can't and won't "put-down," teachers included. Since he tends to instigate conflict among his classmates, without ever becoming directly involved, he is a constant classroom management concern. He is good in all subjects as well as being athletically and musically inclined. His grades are very good.

FRANKLIN: Franklin, not "Frank" but <u>FRANKLIN</u>, is upper-middle class, an academically good student, and the class pest. He always finishes his work quickly and accurately. Then he proceeds to pester, tease, and generally annoy his slower working classmates in a wide variety of imaginative ways. All of his grades are good. He is especially good in math and science. Because of both is academic quickness and his disruptive nuisance behavior, it is a constant strain on his teachers' resources to keep him meaningfully busy.

GEORGE: George is of Appalachian descent, and poor. He is considered a compulsive their and liar. He will steal anything, from his classmates' pencils, to library books obtainable by loan, to the principal's car keys. He steals even though he gets caught frequently and has no apparent use for many of the things stolen. He also lies about anything and even in the most obvious situations. He presents no special classroom management problem other than requiring constant watching by his teachers. His grades are generally good, especially those in math and physical education.

MARCIA: Marcia is a visually and orthopedically impaired youngster who has been mainstreamed into regular class for homeroom and math. She is generally quiet in class and presents no classroom management problem other than that resulting from her classmates inordinate desire to assist her at even the simplest tasks. Her grades are very low overall, except for math where she is especially good.

HELEN: Helen is very sexually precocious and also the self-styled class feminist. She can often be found competing with boys and insultingly putting them down when she has an audience. On the other hand, she has been found several times attempting to seduce some isolated boy into a compromising situation. She has good grades in all subjects and presents no real behavior management problem beyond that already described.

EDDIE: Eddie is a student with an acute sensitivity, awareness, and pride in his "blackness." He is middle-class economically, and is also the son of a man who was deeply involved in and committed to the so-called "Black Revolutionary Movement of the 1960s. He is so acutely sensitive to racial

41

overtones that he insists that the "colored paper" used in art projects be called "construction paper." While all of his grades are good, he is especially strong in language arts, reading, and social studies. The only classroom management issues presented involve his tendency to constantly ask challenging questions and to "correct" his classmates as well as teachers.

ELAINE: Elaine is the "class clown" variety. While she is a very bright and capable student, she appears to prefer investing her energy into making her classmates laugh. She will do anything for a laugh and never seems to satisfy her appetite for attention. While she is very capable in math, science, and social studies, her grades are only fair. She needs and, in fact, demands constant attention, supervision, and structure from her teachers.

FREDDIE: Freddie is of bi-racial parentage and an only child. He tends to be the class bully who with little and ususally no provovation threatens as well as actually beats up on classmates. This bully behavior is most confined to his interactions with others during math and physical education. His bully behavior is seen as a response to the perception of competition or as a strategy to discourage competition in these areas. Overall, his grades are low with the exception of math and physical education. This student requires constant watching by his teachers.

PAULA: Paula is a student who is non-descript. She is that "invisible" child who is easy to forget and overlook because "nothing" is her most striking characteristic. She does nothing outstandingly well nor poor; in fact, most of the time she plain does nothing at all. Her non-performance is so inobstrusive as to defy any notice of her teachers most of the time. Her grades are fair to average.

CAROL: Carol comes from a long line of prominent and wealthy relatives. Her grades are generally good and especially so in language arts, reading, and music. She tends to be verbally abusive and insensitive to classmates whom she considers her social inferiors. She also tends to exhibit a condescending attitude in her interaction with her teachers.

MIA: Mia is a "Shrinking Violet" who is very reluctant to socially interact. She never volunteers nor participates without coaxing. Her grades are average to good; she is especially strong in spelling. She requires a lot of attention, effort, and encouragement from teachers, who could easily ignore her if they didn't make a conscious effort to include her.

WHAT WILL YOU DO WITH THE REJECTS?

Introduction: In the simulation activity involving choosing 15 class members, you did not select seven children based on some characteristic of the child. For this follow-up activity, please write a brief statement answering the following:

1.   Why do you feel that the child would not "fit" in your group?

2.   Why do you think the child is the way she/he is?

3.   What services do you feel the child needs?

4.   How would you go about asking a principal or supervisor to move the child from your class?

5.   If the child could not be moved from your class, what techniques could you use to deal with the problem?

Section 3:

Language Diversity in the U.S.

Conflicts and Commitments

Introduction

Bilingual education in the United States is undergoing great scrutiny. It is one of the most important, dynamic and dramatic reform movemens in the history of American public education. Although language diversity is a reality in this country, the method(s) of dealing with it vary greatly. Simply bilingual education is not without controversy.

We are in the midst of "hard times" in this country, when one thinks of double digit inflation and the recent "cut-backs" in programs... Bilingual education being one of them. These movements have serious implications for minorities (linguistical-ly and culturally distinct students) for the majority (monolin-gual students), for present and future teachers, and for those educational entities responsible for pre-service and in-service teacher training.

Section 3 is intended to provide you with a variety of viewpoints on the educational needs of linguistically different students and the proposed method(s) of addressing those needs. Bilingual education is a very complex and highly controversial

45

issue today. We as educators, need to come to some understanding of where WE stand on these important concerns in order to deal most effectively with the linguistically different student.

A Fable

In a house there was a cat, always ready to run after a mouse, but with no luck at all.

One day, in the usual chase the mouse found its way into a little hole and the cat was left with no alternative than to wait hopefully outside.

A few moments later the mouse heard a dog barking and automatically came to the conclusion that if there was a dog in the house, the cat would have to go. So he came out only to fall in the cat's grasp.

"But where is the dog?"—asked the trembling mouse.

"There isn't any dog—it was only me imitating a barking dog," explained the happy cat, and after a pause added, "My dear fellow, if you don't speak at least two languages, you can't get anywhere nowadays."

Reprinted from *BBC Modern English*, Vol. 2, No. 10, p. 34, December 1976.

INTRODUCTION

In the United States today, there are millions of children
and adults trying to live and function within a cultural and linguistic mainstream new to them. For the adults who are already oriented to a way of life and whose range of responses is organized
around familiar ones, the process of adapting to a new environment
can be very difficult. For the children who are thrust into a new
set of living and learning conditions before they have fully learned
the language and ways of their native culture, the results can be
devastating. The new setting threatens and often destroys the
children's personal growth and self-concepts.

For the children, the transition from home to school is often
drastic and brings about even greater feelings of insecurity. The
children seldom know English when they enter school and thereby
lack the most important tool for learning: Language. They are
caught between two cultures and two languages, neither of which
seems readily accessible.[1]

The United States has always had minority groups with different
languages and cultures. In assessing the need for any special
educational assistance for limited English speaking students today, it is useful to understand the evolutionaly pattern of language
treament that has occurred in this country:

1. From 1789 to 1880 there was no explicit designation of English
   as the official language and there was a great tolerance for
   the use of other languages.

2. From 1880 until World War II, the official designation of
   English at the state and federal level with the clear use of
   these language requirements was to exclude and discriminate
   against various minorities and immigrant groups.

3. Since World War II, and especially in the last fifteen years,
   the relaxation of these requirements and even the encouragement
   of the use of other languages took place.

   *Note: For a brief historical survey of these three distinct
   periods of language treatment in the United States see:
   Rodriguez, Fred. "The Treatment of Different Languages
   in the United States – An Historical Glance." Lucas
   Brothers Publishing Co., Columbia, Missouri. 1979.

47

LEGISLATION AND LEGAL IMPLICATIONS

The need to review and investigate the educational history
of legal issues in regard to the limited English speaking student
is essential. This matter has attracted the attention, not only of
educators, but of legislators and jurists as well. From an educational standpoint and its societal ramifications, Justice J.
Hufstedler points out that," These children are not separated from
their English speaking classmates by.... walls or brick and mortar
but by the language barrier" (Lau v. Nichols).

To this Gaardner adds: The language barrier in school is one
strong reinforcing element, for if ... the all-powerful school...
rejects the mother-tongue of an entire group of children, it can
be expected to affect seriously and adversely those children's
concept of their parents, their homes, and of themselves.[2]

As early as 1923, the Supreme Court in Meyer v. Nebraska
struck down a restriction in the teaching of modern foreign languages
as an infringement of liberty "to acquire useful knowledge."

Historically, the federal government has played a limited role
in the financing of public instruction. By the middle of the 1960's
however, the pattern was to change drastically. This shift is
clearly demonstrated with the introduction and passage of the
Elementary and Secondary Education Act of 1965. Title I education
programs which were created under this new program were intended to
provide additional financial assistance to meet the particular
educational needs of impoverished and "educationally deprived"
school age children. The Elementary and Secondary Education Act su-
pports relevant educational reform in its declaration of policy
statement in that it provides recognition for the need of other
types of educational and instructional approaches regarding the
educational needs of students of limited English speaking abilities
and/or students from low-income family backgrounds.

Proper implementation of federally sponsored educational programs was aided and regulated by the federal guidelines of the Civil
Rights Act of 1964. Section 601 of the Civil Rights Act provides
that:
> No person in the United States shall, on the grounds of
> race, color, or national origin be excluded from participa-
> tion in, be denied the benefits of, or be subjected to dis-
> crimination under any program or activity receiving fed-
> eral financial assistance.[3]

The organized political pressure of the 1960's resulted in recognition of the special educational needs of many limited English

English speaking students in American public schools. The efforts of this awarenes- culminated in 1967 with the introduction of the first bilingual education bill ever to be considered by the Congress. Final passage of the bilingual bill was to create Title VII of the Elementary and Secondary Ed. Act of 1965.

Section (702) of the Bilingual Education Act Asserts:
1. that there are large numbers of children of limited English speaking ability;
2. that many of such children have a cultural heritage which differs from that of English speaking persons;
3. that the use of a child's language and cultural heritage is the primary means by which a child learns; and
4. that, therefore, large numbers of children of limited English speaking ability have educational needs which can be met by the use of bilingual educational methods and techniques;
5. that, in addition, all children benefit through the fullest utilization of multiple language and cultural resources.

Furthermore:
Congress hereby declares it to be the policy of the United States to (1) encourage the establishment and operation of educational programs using bilingual educational methods and techniques and (2) for that purpose, provide financial assistance to local educational agencies in order to enable such agencies to carry out such programs in elementary, including preschool, and secondary schools which are designed to meet the educational needs of such children.[3]

LEGAL IMPLICATIONS

The force which may have brought about the greatest gains for bilingual/bicultural education, and to which such national entities as the NEA and the Civil Rights Commission contributed, were the education lawsuits that challenged the disproportionate placement of Mexican American and other linguistically and culturally distinct children in EMR classes.

In considering the developmental history of bilingual education, it is important that the teacher, teacher-to-be, counselor, administrator, and teacher educator be aware of the significan lawsuits. These lawsuits were the first legal challenges to early testing, standardized tests, the selection process, and the caliber of instruction in EMR classes. In essence, they found that standardized tests were used to measure the capacity to know and speak English rather than a child's general achievement.

Diana v. State Board of Education was argued in federal court.
The judgement of the court was that Mexican American and Chinese
speaking children already in classes for the mentally retarded must
be retested in their primary language and must be reevaluated only
as to their achievement on nonverbal tests or sections of tests.[4]

Although this case was concerned with EMR classes, it became
clear that it was the teachers, counselors and administrators who
were referring linguistically and culturally distinct children to
such classes because, to quote one administrator, "We just do not
know what to do with them." The basis for most of the judgments
which placed these children in EMR classes was their inability to
speak or to function well in English, which had nothing to do with
their mental or psychological capacities. It was evident that in
too many instances the language and culture of the schools could
not or would not adapt to the language and culture of a distinct
community of pupils.

The EMR lawsuits made their own impact on educational reform.
Specifically, they contributed to acceptance of the notion that
there was a serious problem, that it started very early in the
child's life, that it had to do mainly with language and culture,
and that what the schools were doing was not working for the linguistically and culturally distinct child. If anything, what the
schools were doing was educationally and psychologically damaging
to the child, and a new educational strategy had to be developed.
The EMR cases, especially Diana v. Board of Education, led to the
development of what is commonly referred to today as the May 25th
Memorandum.

The May 25th Memorandum (1970), Office for Civil Rights, is
the official policy of the Office for Civil Rights regarding responsibility of the public schools to provide for the educational
needs of linguistically and culturally distinct students, in com-
pliance with the 1964 Civil Rights Act and the 1968 elaboration.
The four points of the memorandum are as follows:

1. Where inability to speak and understand the English
   language excludes national origin-minority-group children
   from effective participation in the educational program
   offered by a school district, the district must take affirmative steps to rectify the language deficiency in order
   to open its instructional program to these students.

2. School districts must not assign national origin-minority
   group students to classes for the mentally retarded on the
   basis of criteria which essentially measure or evaluate
   English language skills; nor may school districts deny
   national origin-minority group children access to college

preparatory courses on the basis directly related to the failure of the school system to inculcate English language skills.

3. Any ability grouping or tracking system employed by the school system to deal with the special language skill needs of national origin-minority group children must be designed to meet such language skill needs as soon as possible and must not operate as an educational dead end or permanent track.

4. School districts have the responsibility to adequately notify national origin-minority group parent(s) of school activities which are called to the attention of other parents. Such notice in order to be adequate may have to be provided in a language other than English.[5]

A number of education lawsuits in addition to the EMR cases have contributed significantly to the rise of bilingual programs and sensitivity to the special educational nees of linguistically and culturally distinct students in this country.

References:

1. Board of Education of the City of Chicago, A Comprehensive Design for Bilingual/Bicultural Education (Washington: Department of Government Funded Programs, 1975, p.3

2. Equal Educational Opportunity Commission, "EEOC Files Four Job Discrimination Suits Against Employers and Unions, Press Release, November 8, 1973.

3. Elementary and Secondary Education Act of 1965, Bilingual Education Act of 1967 (Washington, D.C.,: Government Printing Office, 1967.

4. Diana v. State Board of Education, C70-37-REP, Soledad, California.

5. May 25th Memorandum, Office for Civil Rights (Washington, D.C.: Government Printing Office, 1970), Appendix H, p. 335.

History of Equal Educational Opportunity

In recent years, the Supreme Court has limited state discretion in formulating educational policy when it conflicts with that equalizing role of the public schools. Thus, the Supreme Court established a constitutional mandate of equal educational opportunity years ago when it declared in Brown v. Board of Education (1954) that the opportunity to an education is a right which must be made available to all races on equal terms. In a more recent case, Swann v. Board of Education (1971), the Supreme Court reiterated that segregation based on race was a denial of the equal protection clause under the Fourteenth Amendment.[1]

The Lau v. Nichols decision of the Supreme Court in January 1974, represented a key change in constitutional doctrine and is shown in Appendix A. The Court declared that school districts receiving Federal money were in violation of Title VI of the Civil Rights Act of 1964 if they did not offer some form of special instruction and provide an equal educational opportunity to students with limited English-speaking ability. The Court did not indicate what specific kind of instruction should be provided, nor did it indicate that there was any Federal obligation to provide such instruction. The Court continued by stating that Federally-funded schools must provide special training for limited-English speakers. This special training, however, was not to represent permanent tracking or an educational dead-end. In effect, the Court now had extended interpretation of Federal civil rights laws prohibiting discrimination on the basis of race or religion to encompass Federally-funded schools which had failed to meet the needs of linguistic minorities. In the Lau v. Nichols decision, the Court declared that simply providing limited-English speakers with the same facilities, textbooks, teachers and curriculum as the majority language student did not represent equality in treatment.

Given the controversy surrounding bilingual-bicultural education, the estimated five million limited English-speaking children who need special language programs and the Supreme Court's recent decisions, it is essential to understand the most commonly used approaches to the education of these students.

Development of the Concept of Bilingual-Bicultural
Education: The Different Approaches

Bilingual-bicultural education competes with other approaches in meeting the needs of limited English-speaking students. In recent years, the bilingual-bicultural approach has developed in response to dissatisfaction with the limitations of other approaches. The U.S. Commission on Civil Rights stated that the three basic approaches generally used to teach limited

52

and non-native speakers of English in the primary grades are the remedial, the English-as-a-Second-Language (ESL) and the bilingual-bicultural approach.[3]

The Remedial Approach

The remedial approach is defined as "special instruction intended to overcome in part or in whole any particular deficiency of a pupil not due to inferior general ability, for example, remedial reading instruction for pupils with reading difficulties."[4] The remedial approach was used widely prior to the adoption of ESL and bilingual-bicultural programs, and it still is being implemented today. Remedial programs generally have been associated with the tracking system and educational programs devised for slow learners.[5] Remedial programs contain few positive aspects. The remedial approach often assumed that the educational gap between native and non-native speakers can be closed by placing the limited English-speaking child in classes for slow learners where English is still the medium of instruction. The remedial approach does not utilize the native language nor does it seek to utilize cultural characteristics of linguistic minorities.[6]

According to current research, in some remedial programs, linguistic minority children are removed from the regular school program and placed in programs designated for low-intelligence children.[7] The U.S. Commission on Civil Rights found that, in some cases, these minority children were placed in classes for the mentally retarded solely because of their inability to speak English. In the primary schools, the children were placed in slow groups while at the secondary level they were channeled into vocational education courses.[8]

The ESL Approach

The English-as-a-Second-Language (ESL) approach is defined as a program designed to teach English to non-native speakers without the use of the native language as a medium of instruction.[9] In the 1960s, there was an increased realization that linguistic minority children needed more than remedial programs if they were to have an equal opportunity for success in school.[10] Moreover, the 1967 Bilingual Education Act provided funds and a Federal stimulus to support ESL and bilingual-bicultural programs which incorporated the children's native language and culture as an integral part of the daily instruction.[11]

In the late 1950s and early 1960s, the increase in popular usage of the ESL approach was seen. This was due to the much publicized success of the audio-lingual method used first by the Army Language Schools and then adapted to the public school classroom by foreign language teachers. The audio-lingual ESL method was based on the hypothesis that oral language skills must precede formal instruction in reading and writing.[12]

A closer look at the ESL approach shows that "in a typical ESL program, children receive all subject area instruction in English but are 'pulled out' of class for special English language skills training."[13] ESL programs emphasize the formal learning of the oral language skills of speaking and listening comprehension. The goal of ESL training is training on the language elements causing the greatest difficulty.[14] Most important, according to a footnote in the U.S. Commission on Civil Rights Report.[15]

Because the term ESL is used to describe a course designed to teach English skills, it is also a component of all bilingual-bicultural programs. The terms "ESL approach" is used to indicate the use of ESL instruction within a monolingual English curriculum. The methodology used for both can be identical, but the content of instruction will differ depending on the amount and type of English learning which takes place outside the ESL class.[16]

The U.S. Commision on Civil Rights concluded in 1975 that ESL approach is useful only in communities where children receive substantial exposure to English outside the classroom. In addition, the ESL approach can be beneficial only in communities where the child can develop a positive attitude toward learning English while maintaining pride in the native language and culture.[17] The results of learning a second language through a total immersion approach were observed by Lambert and Tucker in a study conducted of English-speaking youngsters who, although a

54

linguistic minority in their French-speaking community in Montreal, represented the local economic elite as well as Canada's majority culture. Lambert and Tucker found that total immersion in French produced no retardaton in English comprehension and these students performed as well as their French-speaking counterparts on reading tests in French. In addition, Tucker stated in an interview that the English-speaking children had the added advantage of being able to function in two languages and cultures.[18]

The Bilingual-Bicultural Approach

Growing out of the dissatisfaction with the other approaches, bilingual-bicultural education contains different cultural and educational components. The U.S. Commission on Civil Rights defines bilingual-bicultural education as a comprehensive approach which goes beyond the mere imparting of English skills.[19] Thus, the third approach, bilingual-bicultural education uses the native language as part of the instructional program while English is being introduced. While there are many models of bilingual-bicultural programs, a major compoenent of all is the "inclusion in the curriculum of the child's historical, literary, and cultural traditions for the purposes of strengthening identity and sense of belonging and for making the instructional program easier to grasp."[20] The programs vary according to the time the native language is maintained as in integral part of the curriculum. Moreover, researchers in bilingual-bicultural education such as Saville and Troike argue that bilingual-bicultural education fosters development of a positive self-concept which is essential to a successful school experience for any child.[21]

In addition, in the bilingual-bicultural approach, content areas are studied in two languages, the native language and English. The program may include part or all of the subjects in a school curriculum which are usually taught at each grade level. Programs also may include study of the history and culture associated with the native language to develop and maintain children's self-esteem and cultural pride. The basic goal of bilingual-bicultural programs is to enable children from a limited English-speaking environment to progress at the same rate and at as high a level of academic achievement as children from an English-speaking environment. This is particularly true for foreign students who enter schools in the United States at a later age. Bilingual-bicultural education allows the student to increase skills through native language instruction and to transfer the content areas to English without a long period elapsing while the student learns English.

Even within the bilingual-bicultural approach there are a variety of different program models. According to Gonzalez, the most common exposition of differences has been to describe a dichotomy between the transitional and maintenance approaches. The transitional approach means the sole program objective is to achieve English language competency, and the method of special instruction continues only to that point. The object of the maintenance approach is to maintain the native language and native culture beyond the point of English language competence.[22]

Gonzalez also distinguished additional subdivisions in approaches used, and analysis which illustrates the complexity of the current policy debate. The models Gonzalez examined were labeled: the "ESL/Bilingual Transitional Program," the "Bilingual Maintenance Program," the "Bilingual/Bicultural Maintenance Program," the "Bilingual/Bicultural Restorative Program" used in those cases where native language proficiency has been lost, and the "Culturally Pluralistic Program" for both native and non-native English speakers.[23]

These differing program models reflect the range of opinion concerning the use and implementation of bilingual-bicultural education. In the narrowest interpretation, bilingual-bicultural education is designed merely to allow the limited-English speaker the opportunity to gain English language skills. The broadest interpretation manifests the belief that bilingual-bicultural education should be for everyone, that all can benefit from bilingual-bicultural training and that the goal is the creation of a bilingual-bicultural society. There has been substantial disagreement over the proper approach in educating linguistic minorities. Negative views have been expressed by educators and taxpayers on the issue of the costs of bilingual-bicultural education.[24]

Bibliography

[1]Swann v. Board of Education, 402 U.S. 1, 5, 9 (1971).

[2]Lau v. Nichols, 414 U.S. 563 (1974).

[3]U.S., Commission on Civil Rights, The Excluded Students, Report III: Educational Practices Affecting Mexican Americans in the Southwest (Washington, D.C.: U.S. Government Printing Office, May 1972), p. 48.

[4]Carter V. Good, ed., Dictionary of Education, 3rd ed. (New York: McGraw-Hill Book Company, 1973), p. 590.

[5]U.S., Commission on Civil Rights, The Excluded Students, Report III, p. 28.

[6]Swanson, "Bilingual Education," p. 86.

[7]Ibid.

[8]U.S., Commission on Civil Rights, Toward Quality Education for Mexican Americans, Report VI: Mexican American Education Study (Washington, D.C.: U.S. Government Printing Office, February 1974), pp. 71-72.

[9]Mary Finocchiaro, Teaching English as a Second Language (New York: Harper and Row, Publishers, 1969), p. 447.

[10]U.S., Commission on Civil U.S., Commission on Civil Rights, A Better Chance to Learn, p. 19.

[11]Ibid., p. 20.

[12]Gonzalez, "Coming of Age in Bilingual Education," pp. 7-8.

[13]U.S., Commission on Civil Rights, A Better Chance to Learn, p. 22.

[14]Ibid., p. 23.

[15]Ibid., p. 22.

[16]Ibid., p. 28.

[17]Interview with G. Richard Tucker, Professor, McGill University, Montreal, Canada, Washington, D.C., 13 August 1976; Wallace E. Lambert and G. Richard Tucker, Bilingual Education of Children: TheSt. Lambert Experiment (Towley, Massachusetts: Newbury House Publishers, 1972), pp. 152-153.

[18]U.S., Commission on Civil Rights, A Better Chance to Learn, p. 3.

[19]Ibid., p. 29.

[20]Muriel R. Saville and Rudolph C. Troike, A Handbook of Bilingual Education (Washington, D.C.: Teachers of English to Speakers of Other Languages, 1971), p. 21.

[21]U.S., Commission on Civil Rights, A Better Chance to Learn, p. 29.

[22]Gonzalez, "Coming of Age in Bilingual Education," pp. 14-15.

[23]Ibid.

[24]U.S., Congress, Senate, Committee on Labor and Public Welfare, Education Legislation, 1973, Hearings, S. 1539, p. 2932; Stephen S. Rosenfeld, "Bilingualism and the Melting Pot," Washington Post, 27 September 1974, p. A18.

BILINGUAL PROGRAMS SPONSORED BY THE DEPARTMENT OF EDUCATION

(Forty-six Languages Represented)
(1980)

NATIVE AMERICAN LANGUAGES (INDIAN)

Apache
Cherokee
Choctaw
Cree
Crow
Eelaponke
Havasupai
Keresan
Lakota
Miccosukee-Seminole
Mohawk
Navajo
Northern Cheyenne
Paiute
Papago
Passamaquoddy
Seminole-Creek
Tewa
Ute
Walapai

(ESKIMO)

Aleut
Central Yupik
Gwichin
Inupik

EUROPEAN LANGUAGES

French
Canadian French
Haitian Creole
Greek
Italian
Pennsylvania Dutch (German)
Polish
Portuguese
Spanish
Russian
Yiddish

OTHER LANGUAGES

Arabic
Hebrew
Punjabi (India)
Samoan
Cambodian
Chinese
Ilocano (Philippines)
Japanese
Korean
Tagalog (Phillippines)
Vietnamese

*Source: Department of Education

Note: Approximately 325 million dollars from various sources of the federal government support many of the above bilingual programs in the country.

60

QUESTIONS FOR DISCUSSION

1. What do you consider the advantages and disadvantages of Bilingual Education?

_____

_____

_____

_____

_____

_____

_____

2. What do you consider the advantages and disadvantages of an ESL Program?

_____

_____

_____

_____

_____

_____

3. As a prospective classroom teacher, what are your opinions/ ideas in regards to meeting the needs of linquistically different students. In other words, what should the public schools endorse?

_____

_____

_____

_____

_____

_____

_____

4. The funding of programs for meeting the needs of limited
    English speaking students should be from:

    _____ Federal government

    _____ State government

    _____ Local communities

    _____ None of the above

    Why? Defend your answer.

    _____

    _____

    _____

    _____

    _____

    _____

    _____

5. Do you think there should be an Amendment to the Constitution
    declaring English as the National language in the United
    States?

    Yes _____   No _____   Don't really know _____

    Explain your response:

    _____

    _____

Section 4:

Legal Issues

In Equal Educational Opportunity

Laws and Case Examples

Introduction

In school districts all over the country, school boards and administrators have fired teachers because they belonged to an unpopular organization, because they publicly critized their school system or for a variety of other reasons. In most cases, the people involved chose not to fight for their legal rights.

In thousands of schools, the rights of teachers and students are violated on a daily basis, and just as frequently, teachers themselves unwittingly break the law and place themselves in legal jeopardy. The common thread in all these situations is an ignorance of the law. Simply stated, most teachers are unaware of either their OWN legal rights and responsibilities or those of their STUDENTS.

Although it impossible to review in section 4 all the court rulings and federal laws pertaining to teacher and student rights, it is important that YOU be aware of both your legal rights and responsibilities as a teacher as well as those of your students. The following will test your legal knowledge regarding a number of common situations based on court cases or a federal regulation. But, first a brief review of those laws is given.

63

WHAT LAWS AFFECT SCHOOLS

There are nine United States anti-discrimination laws and one Presidential executive order enforced by different agencies and requiring different remedies if violations are proven. However, they are very similar in the educational activities which they affect and the types of discrimination they prohibit. They are as follows:

1. Title VI of the Civil Rights Act of 1964 (P.L. 88-352): prohibits discrimination on the basis of race, color or national origin against students of any school receiving federal assistance. (OCR/U.S.E.D.)*

2. Title IX of the Education Amendments of 1972 (P.L. 92-318): prohibits discrimination on the basis of sex against students and any employee of a school receiving federal financial assistance. (OCR/U.S.E.D.)

3. Title VII of the Civil Rights Act of 1964 (P.L. 88-352): prohibits discrimination against employees on the basis of race, color, national origin, religion or sex by any employer in the United States who employs 15 or more people. This also includes employment agencies and labor unions. (EEOC)

4. Equal Pay Act, as amended in 1972 (P.L. 88-38): prohibits discrimination on the basis of sex in wages and fringe benefits by any employer in the United States. (DOL)

5. The Education for All Handicapped Children Act (P.L. 94-142), U.S.C. 1411, 1976: provides federal financial assistance to schools in educating young people between six and 21 years of age who have been properly identified and evaluated to be in the targeted categories of: special education, hearing or speech impaired, visually or orthopedically handicapped, emotionally disturbed or specific learning disabilities. The law provides a state, between 1977 and 1981, with assistance equal to from five to 40 percent of the state's average per pupil expenditure for these young people 'if the state follows the required identification, evaluation and programming of the law. The law requires that stdents with a handicap be educated in the "most integrated setting" appropriate. The school must provide each student with an individual education program. Schools are required to search for students with a handicap, rather than waiting for students to identify themselves to the school.

* Enforcing agencies: OCR/U.S.E.D. = Office for Civil Rights/ United States Education Department; EEOC = Equal Employment Opportunities Commission; DOL = Department of Labor.

The local education agency, in most cases the school district, is financially responsible for providing all necessary programming for the handicapped student. (OCR/U.S.E.D.)

6. The Vocational Education Act of 1963, as amended by the Education Amendments of 1976 (P.L. 94-482): requires states to make new efforts to overcome sex discrimination and stereotyping in vocational education. (OCR/U.S.E.D.)

7. Executive Order 11246 amended by 11375 (1968): prohibits discrimination against employees on the basis of race, color, religion, sex or national origin in all schools with federal contracts or subcontracts of $10,000 or more. These orders also require written affirmative action programs for schools holding federal contracts of $50,000 or more. (OCR/U.S.E.D.)

8. The Rehabilitation Act of 1973 (P.L. 93-112): promotes and expands the opportunities available to individuals with handicaps. Section 502 requires complete accessibility in all buildings constructed after 1968 and financed with federal funds. Section 503 requires federal contracts valued over $2,500 to include affirmative action and nondiscrimination clauses. Section 504 and its regulations provide equal educational opportunity for "otherwise qualified handicapped individuals" in all educational programs. Equal Educational Opportunity requires program accessibility, identification of needs for educational assistance and provision for financial assistance to allow participation in the school. (OCR/U.S.E.D.)

9. Pregnancy Discrimination Act (P.L. 95-555), 1978, an amendment to Title VII of the Civil Rights Act of 1964: makes clear that discrimination on the basis of pregnacy, childbirth or related medical conditions constitutes unlawful sex dscrimination under Title VII. (EEOC)

10. Age Discrimination in Employment Act as amended in 1978 prohibits employers, employment agencies and labor organizations with 20 or more employees from basing hiring decisions on a person's age when the person's age is between 40 and 70 unless an age limit is a necessary qualification for job performance. (DOL; OCR/U.S.E.D.)

Federal laws are accompanied by regulations formulated by the agencies which enforce the laws. Federal regulations are enforced by the Office for Civil Rights/United States Education Department; Equal Educational Opportunities Commission; and the

Department of Labor. These regulations have the force of law, unless they are found by a court to be beyond the scope or intention of the law. They should be followed by educational institutions and staff in the same manner as the law. If a regulation is violated by an instituion, the enforcement agencies of the federal government will consider the law to be violated.

Adapted from: Teacher Standards and Practices Commission, Discriminaton and the Oregon Educator, second edition (Salem, Oregon: TSPC, 1980), pp. 4-5.

FEDERAL LAW SUMMARY SHEET

Law or Executive Order	Prohibits	Covers
Equal Pay Act, 1963	Sex discrimination (in pay only)	Employees
Vocational Education Act, 1963	Sex discrimination in vocational education	Students
Title VI, Civil Rights Act of 1964	Race, color and national origin discrimination	Students
Title VII, Civil Rights Act of 1964	Race, sex, color, national origin and religious discrimination	Employees
Executive Order 11246 (as amended by E.O. 11375), 1968	Race, sex, color national origin and religious discrimination	Employees
Title IX, Education Amendments of 1972	Sex discrimination	Employees students
Rehabilitation Act, 1973, Section 504	Handicapped discrimination	Employees students
Public Law 94-142, 1976	Handicapped discrimination	Students
Pregnancy Discrimination Act, 1978	Sex discrimination (pregnancy)	Employees
Age Discrimination in Employment Act, amended 1978	Age discrimination	Employees

67

CASE ANALYSIS #1

Mr. Ramirez, a science teacher at Oregon Valley High School, has approached the principal about the state adopted textbooks used in his classes. They are biased against women and minorities in his estimation. The accomplishments of these groups are not recognized, the language is sexist, and accurate representation of the American family is not present. Mr. Ramirez demands that funds be made available to provide him and other teachers with materials that are representative.

What laws, if any apply here?
Does the teacher have any legal rights here?

CASE ANALYSIS #2

The father of an eighth grade girl has requested that his daughter be removed from coeducational physical education classes because her wearing the prescribed gym shorts and short in a coed setting violates the family's religious beliefs. The school district has recently made the required physical education classes coeducational.

Can the District legally exempt the girl from P.E. or are there other althernatives available?

What laws, if any, apply in this situation?

CASE ANALYSIS #3

Ms. Red Bird, an experienced social studies teacher with an outstanding record of performance, has recently moved to the area included in District 41. She is interested in obtaining a position teaching social studies at the junior high school or senior high school level. She obtained an interview with a member of the District personnel office. The interviewer reviewed her record and recommendations, commented on them favorably, but indicated it would not be possible to offer her a position in the area of social studies since the open position required a teacher who could also serve as coach for boys' basketball. Although Ms. Red Bird said she enjoyed sports and was willing to take a course in coaching, the interviewer was firm about needing an experienced coach.

Is this legal?
Which laws, if any, are relevant to this situation?

CASE ANALYSIS #4

East High School provides a variety of academic and extracurricular activities for its 1,200 students. In the wake of a 1980 desegregation order, more than 500 black student from West High School, which has been attended primarily by black students, were reassigned to East High School. All black students are automatically assigned to one semester of remedial English and must demonstrate proficiency in English before they may enroll in other English courses. There is no equivalent requirement for non-black students.

- Does the English requirement for blacks violate any antidiscrimination laws or decisions of the federal courts?

  Yes (___)   No (___)

  Which ones?

CASE ANALYSIS #5

A tenured kindergarten teacher in Midlands School District has been informed that her contract will not be renewed next year because of her refusal to teach certain parts of the required curriculum. Ms. Herriot, a Jehovah's Witness, plans to file suit against the District, claiming her rights to religious freedom have been violated. Her religious beliefs prohibit her teaching students the pledge of allegiance, patriotic songs, or conducting activities connected with holidays, such as Halloween, Thanksgiving and Columbus Day. Ms. Herriot believes these activities are forms of idolatry and worship of artificial images banned by the Bible.

- Do you think Ms. Herriot's constitutional rights are being violated? On what basis would you argue this case?

  Yes ____   No ____

- Can a District waive the responsibility to teach the required curriculum to accommodate a teacher's personal beliefs?

  Yes ____   No ____   ? ____

- Would you, if you were the School Board, renew her contract to teach?

  Yes ____   No ____   ? ____

69

CASE ANALYSIS #6

May Chao, a Laotian student, has been placed in the Mitchell Elementary School program for handicapped children. Her foster family is complaining to the school that they con't believe she is either physically or mentally handicapped. The teacher, who had May placed in the program for hearing impaired, explained that he felt May should stay in the program until she learns English well enough to transfer to a regular class. The teacher believes that this environment will allow the child to make the most rapid progress as there is a low teacher/pupil ratio, time for individual attention, and simple object identification programs in sign language. The teacher in the class has agreed to audibly instruct May, while she is teaching the other children sign language.

- What, if any, laws are involved here?
- If you were the administration, how would you handle the situation?

CASE ANALYSIS #7

One of Merrymount's shop instructors intends to file a grievance concerning his desire not have female students in his Tool & Die Making course. He has already refused one junior girl admission to the class, and she has complained to the administration. The shop instructor claims that female students can't lift the dies, weighing 70-90 lbs., onto machines used in his class. In addition, no shop would hire a woman to work in this type of job. The shops in the community also subsidize the school's course by providing equipment for use in the class. The instructor says the female students could be accommodated by another teacher in the department who has agreed to take them in his class. If the shop instructor has to take the girls, he says he will have to lower his professional teaching standards for the whole group. The administraton has yet to act on either complaint.

- What laws, if any, are violated?

70

CASE ANALYSIS #8

Ty Valley High School has a dress code that was democratically ratified by 70 percent of the student body and that prohibits "extreme nonconformity" in personal appearance. The principal has used this code to send the following students home:

1. Bill who wears an earring in his left ear
2. Fred who has shoulder-length hair
3. Sandra who wore a T-shirt with a political statement on it

- Is the dress code in violation of the rights of students?
  Yes _____ No _____

- Has the principal acted in a way that violates rights of certain students? Yes _____ No _____

- Is #8 a case of discrimination? Yes _____ No _____

- Which laws, if any, apply to each of the three situations?

CASE ANALYSIS #9

Ms. Johnson has taught for seven years at one of the elementary schools in Hollow Log School District. She is expecting a child in six months. She knows that she can continue teaching throughout her pregnancy if she and her doctor decide it's advisable. She is concerned, however, about how long she can stay at home with the baby after the birth. She would like to stay home at least six or eight weeks. The school district will give her up to a year's leave without pay, but Ms. Johnson's family cannot afford to be without her income for more than two or three weeks.

- Which, if any, discrimination laws apply in this situation?
- Does the school district have any further obligations to Ms. Johnson?

CASE ANALYSIS #10

Jeannette, my 15-year old daughter, is paraplegic and in a wheelchair. Jeannette's teachers never allow her to go outside with the other students, because they are afraid Jeannette will get hurt. Jeannette and another student in a wheelchair are required to eat lunch separately from the other students because the

school says they are too slow in going to the lunchroom. Finally, there is no physical education class provided for my daughter.

· Are there any violations of federal anti-discrimination
  laws?
  Yes _____   No _____

· What are the reasons for your decision? _____
  _____

· What action do you recommend to the school administration?

CASE ANALYSIS #11

Duc Ho, a 14-year old Cambodian refugee, has recently been enrolled in Pleasant Gorge Mid High. He speaks little English but
is adjusting quite well to this small logging community in the
Northwest. He is one of five South East Asian refugees sponsored
by a local church. The Education Service District has assigned
an itinerant, English as a Second Language teacher to work with
Duc Ho on his English skills for twenty minutes on Monday, Wed-
nesday and Friday. Otherwise, he is in regular classes, most of
which are in the industrial arts area. Duc Ho has talked to his
counselor at the Immigration Office about the fact that he is not
learning as much as he should at school.

· What, if anything, is the school obligated to do for
  Duc Ho which they are not doing now?

· What laws, if any, apply in this situation?

From: Teacher Standards and Practices Commission, Discrimina-
           tion and the Oregon Educator, second edition. Salem,
           OR: TSPC, 1980, pp. 32-33.

CASE ANALYSIS #12

A small rural school district, where 95 percent of the population
is Protestant, has for years provided release time for students
to attend religious classes in an empty classroom at one of the
elementary schools. An unsuccessful school board candidate has
lodged a complaint against the District for this practice. The
District argues that no one objected when the church was used by
the school for kindergarten classes and that sending the students
to a church for the voluntary religious class would present a
safety hazard because of busy street.

· What laws, if any, apply to this situation? _____

· Does the District have an obligation to change its practice?

Yes _____ No _____ If so, how? _____

CASE ANALYSIS #13

Kevin is a ninth grader at Six Mile Junior High. He has been playing basketball every year but has recently been outplayed by his team mates who have grown more rapidly than he has. This year the school has a ninth grade volleyball team which thus far has only girls on it. Kevin wants to try out for volleyball because he is sure he could be a star on the team since his years of basketball have given him skills that would be useful in volleyball. With the advent of coed and girls' sports, the coach doesn't know whether Kevin should be able to try out for the team or not.

· What, if any, anti-discrimination laws are applicable here?

· What would you do if you were the coach?

LAW AWARENESS QUIZ

Purpose   The purpose of this quiz is for you to check your
                 own knowledge of anti-discrimination law.

Instructions   Please circle one of the items to indicate whether
                 the practice or procedure described is mandatory
                 ("Must"), permissive ("May"), or prohibited ("Must
                 Not") by law. Use the fourth choice if you don't
                 know what is covered by law.

1.   The school district ____ have a policy which requires teach-
     ers to go on leave after the fourth month of pregnancy.

                 Must   May   Must not   Don't Know

2.   Indochinese refugee students ____ be provided instruction
     in English as well as reading, spelling and other basic
     skills.

                 Must   May   Must not   Don't Know

3.   Teachers ____ use curriculum materials that are biased (do
     not show a fair representation of women and/or minorities).

                 Must   May   Must not   Don't Know

4.   Certified handicapped children ____ have a tailor-made,
     individualized education program.

                 Must   May   Must not   Don't Know

5.   A vocational school ____ limit enrollment of members of one
     sex because of limited availability of job opportunities for
     members of that sex.

                 Must   May   Must not   Don't Know

6.   If a class roster shows that a certain class has a substan-
     tially disproportionate number of students of one sex (e.g.,
     80 percent) enrolled in that class, the school administra-
     tors ____ determine that the disproportion is not a result
     of discrimination.

                 Must   May   Must not   Don't Know

74

7. A school under court order to desegregate _____ require that all incoming minority students attend a basic reading skills course.

      Must   May   Must not   Don't Know

8. A school _____ sponsor separate athletic teams for members of each sex if selection for such teams is based upon competitive skills.

      Must   May   Must not   Don't Know

9. A teacher _____ reserve the use of corporal punishment for boys while finding an alternative punishment for girls.

      Must   May   Must not   Don't Know

10. If parents want to send their children to Christian Bible classes in a neighborhood facility during the school day, the school district _____ allow them.

      Must   May   Must not   Don't Know

11. A school district _____ have different fringe benefit packages for men and women.

      Must   May   Must not   Don't Know

12. Under Title IX a school _____ enroll students in separate physical education classes on the basis of sex.

      Must   May   Must not   Don't Know

Some Thoughts on

Mainstreaming

The term mainstreaming is familiar to educators in connection with efforts to implement PL 94-142, the Education of All Handicapped Children Act of 1975. The act doesn't mention mainstreaming; it simply requires that handicapped students be educated in the Least Restrictive Environment (LRE). In other words, the educational setting must be as normal as possible while meeting students' individual learning needs. This can mean that students remain in special education programs most or all of the time they are in school, because that is the placement most appropriate for them, given their hanicaps. But it can also mean, that depending on the school district's services and the students needs, students may spend most or all of the school day in a regular classroom with special help being provided to the regular classroom teacher.

WHY REGULAR CLASS PLACEMENT?

WHY MAINSTREAMING?

After decades spent designing special education programs, why is it now thought desirable to place exceptional children back into regular classrooms? Should handicapped students have remained in regular classrooms all along? The development of special education has had many beneficial results. For example, it encouraged educators and medical personnel to examine closely both the learning process and learning impairments, promoted awareness of handicaps and of the need to provide appropriate help to the handicapped and their families, and resulted in the formation of parent groups and specialized training programs for parents, paraprofessionals, and teachers.[1] It also brought attention to the lack of materials and techniques for the handicapped and, in many instances, resulted in the development of such materials.

Unfortunately, placement in special education programs also had negative results for many handicapped persons. One of these was the isolation of special students from "normal" peers who could model acceptable behaviors and attitudes. Students became so protected in a special education setting that they were out of touch with the real world in which they would someday function.[2] Another result was the negativism and lowered expectations associated with labeling.

Although mainstreaming will not automatically resolve these problems or guarantee that exceptional students will become functional members of society, it should help them learn to cope with the

77

real world and help non-handicapped students, parents, and professionals learn about and accept individual differences to a greater degree.

WHAT DOES THE RESEARCH SAY ?

According to Dunn,[3] the need and support for integrating handicapped students into the regular classroom rests on seven points.

1. Research shows that, with one exception mentally handicapped students do better in regular classrooms than in special classes. The exception: Peer Acceptance.

2. Labeling and stigmatizing students by sending them to "retarded" classes may prove detrimental to them.

3. Special classes isolate students, preventing meaningful contact that could be helpful both to mentally/physically handicapped and their "normal" peers.

4. Many special classes do not meet- in a real way- the educational and social needs of students.

5. Special classes have an unrealistically high proportion of ethnic minority students and students from low socio-economic backgrounds. (This lack of balance, researchers claim, is the result of a middle class oriented test bias and of environmental deprivation, rather than of actual intellectual inferiority inherent in the schools).

6. Results from standardized I.Q. tests are not sufficient evidence for placing students in special classes.

7. Isolating students in special classes is not in keeping with our democratic philosophy of education.

Mainstreaming is not for everyone; we still need to use self-contained special education classes when they are both the least restrictive and most appropriate setting for a given student. For the mildly handicapped, however demands participation in regular classrooms to some extent. The challenge for all of us is to go beyond the legal requirements by wholly integrating handicapped students into the class, to learn from them and allow them to learn from those without handicaps, providing the most effective education possible while still meeting the conditions imposed by their handicaps - and to do all this willingly.

Anecdotal reports and studies alike indicate that the attitudes of teachers, administrators, and students are crucial elements in the success or difficulties of a mainstreaming effort. Positive attitudes cannot be forced by law; they must be encouraged and carefully supported.

References:

1. Glick, Harriet M., and Schubert, Marsh, "Mainstreaming: An Unmandated Challenge." Educational Leadership, Jan. 1981. p. 326.

2. Dunn, L.M., "Special Education for the Mentally Retarded- Is Much of It Justifiable?" Exceptional Children, 34 (1-68: 5-22).

QUESTIONS FOR DISCUSSION

1. As a prospective classroom teacher, what are your thoughts on the mainstreaming concept?

_____

_____

_____

_____

2. Do you feel your subject area/discipline, grade level is compatable or incompatable with the mainstreaming concept? Why or Why Not?

_____

_____

_____

_____

3. As a prospective classroom teacher, what type(s) of preparation or experiences do you feel "regular" classroom teachers need in their pre-training programs in order for the mainstreaming concept to be successful in the future?

Be specific and provide examples of your response(s).

_____

_____

_____

_____

_____

_____

4. The funding for incorporating the mainstreaming concept
   in our public schools should come from:

   _____ Federal Government

   _____ State Government

   _____ Local Communities

   _____ None of the Above

   Why? Defend your answer.

   _____

   _____

   _____

   _____

   _____

   _____

My Awareness and Understanding of

Child Abuse and Neglect

True or False

T	F	1.	There has been a steady increase in total reports; abuse is reported approximately twice as often as neglect.
T	F	2.	The profile of cases reported over the past three years has been fairly consistent.
T	F	3.	As a result of the figures surrounding child abuse and neglect violence seems to be a pattern rather than a rare phenomenom.
T	F	4.	Survivors of child abuse and neglect will probably be inclined to abuse their own children.
T	F	5.	As of 1979, forty-three states specifically mention educators in in their laws.
T	F	6.	More children in one year die from child maltreatment than most childhood illness.
T	F	7.	All families have the same degree of risk in committing child abuse and neglect.

Multiple Choice

a. 22-45%   1. As a reflection of our cultural
b. 84-97%   acceptance of violence ___ percent
c. 49-66%   of parents use some form of
                    physical punishment.

a. 1-3%　　2. What percent of children in the
b. 5-10%　　　 United States are abused or neg-
c. ½-1½%　　　lected?

a. 35%　　3. What percent of trips to the
b. 50%　　　 hospital are a result of abuse?
c. 25%

a. 5 and 2%　4. _____ percent of girls and _____
b. 10 and 5%　　 percent of boys are sexually
c. 20 and 10%　　molested.

a. 80%　　5. With sexual abuse, _____ percent
b. 50%　　　 of the perpetrators are parents
c. 30%　　　 or guardians.

a. 5%　　6. In 1980, U.S. General Accounting
b. 12%　　　 Office made a report to Congress
c. 22%　　　 on child abuse and neglect which
　　　　　　 stated professionals including
　　　　　　 doctors and teachers - only
　　　　　　 accounted for approximately what
　　　　　　 percent of cases reported.

Child Abuse and Neglect

Child Abuse is a social problem affecting thousands of children each year in all socio-economic levels and from a variety of problem family situations. Recently, there has been a great deal of attention directed toward the problem of child abuse and neglect in the United States. Social service agencies have been aware of the problem of child maltreatment for a number of years. Now medical personnel, educators, law enforcement officers and portions of the general population are becoming aware of child maltreatment and its effects on the child and the family.

Child maltreatment is not only a family problem; nor is it only the problem of those agencies and organizations directly involved in responding to reports of suspected child maltreatment. As with any social problem child maltreatment is a problem of the total community. This community responsibility includes a legal, moral and ethical responsibility for the community as a whole to assume an active role in response to child abuse and neglect.

There are many statistics regarding the incidence of child abuse and neglect.

The national profile of data over the past three years has been fairly consistent. There has been a steady increase in total reports; neglect is reported approximately twice as often as abuse; and 55% of all reported cases are either unsubstaintiated or there are incomplete investigations.

In looking at the data regarding child abuse and neglect estimates range from thousands of cases per year to millions.[1] Child abuse and neglect may be a manifestation of a cultural acceptance of violence as 84-97% of parents use some form of physical punishment with their children. As a result of the figures surrounding child abuse and neglect violence seems to be a pattern rather than a rare phenomenon.[2] Approximately one to three percent of the children are abused or neglected and death results more often from neglect or abuse than from most pediatric illnesses (for example, more children die from abuse than leukemia annually). Hare, reports that "...3½ million children have been kicked, bitten, or punched by their parents...about 2 million have been 'beaten up'... between 1 and 1½ million American children between the ages of 3 and 17 in 1975 have faced parents weilding a gun or knife at them...."[3] The children who survive carry emotional as well as physical scars well into adulthood.

Perhaps the most dismal fact is that the survivors of violent childhoods are inclined to abuse their own children. While there is no consensus as to the causes of child abuse, most authorities agree that the majority of abusers were themselves maltreated. For them, coming of age means confronting the nightmarish possibility that, like carriers of genetically transmitted illness, they may pass on this tragic legacy to the next generation.[4]

There are some demographic characteristics that have been reported. Manual workers, non-whites, families with an unemployed or part time employed father, and families with four or more children appear to be more at risk and reported more frequently.[5] There are more boys under twelve abused than girls while more girls over twelve than boys are abused. Mothers appear to be the perpetrator more often and stepfathers more than stempmothers.[6] It must be pointed out that abusive and neglectful parents come from every walk of life as well as from every ethnic group. This problem has no color, social, economic, religious or political lines.

Of the cases that are reported, a higher number are substantiated when reported by a mandated individual.[7] Of the cases reported, less than 20% need court action. In a hospital emergency room, 50% of the cases are a result of abuse and 30 to 40% of children have as a result physical and/or emotional disability.[8]

The proportion of substaintiated sexual abuse cases appears to be rising. In 1976 the proportion was 3.2%, in 1977, 5.8% and in 1978, 6.2%. Also 15.4%

84

of all substantiated child abuse cases involves
sexual abuse.[9] The parent or guardian is the perpetrator in 80% of the cases. 20% of all girls and
10% of all boys are currently being sexually molested.
In 82.7% of these sexual abuse cases, the abuse is
repeated over a number of years.[10]

Current Laws Pertaining to Child Abuse and Neglect

In 1974, public law 93-247, the Child Abuse
Prevention and Treatment Act, was enacted on the federal level. This act called for the creation of the
National Center on Child Abuse and Neglect (NCCAN)
within the Department of Health Education and Welfare.
This organization was authorized to make grants to the
states and to public and private agencies for programs
directed toward the prevention and treatment of child
abuse and neglect.[11]

An Example of State Laws - The State of Kansas

The Kansas Child Protection Act, K.S.A. 38-716 to
38-724, enacted in 1977 contains a number of provisions regarding the handling of child abuse and
neglect suspected cases.[12] The law begins with a
general policy statement regarding child abuse and
neglect wich reads as follows:

K.S.A. 38-716....."It is the policy of this state
to provide for the protection of children who have
been subject to physical or mental abuse or neglect by
encouraging the reporting of suspected child abuse and
neglect, insuring the thorough and prompt investiga-
tion of these reports and providing preventative and
rehabilitative services where appropriate to abused or
neglected children and their families so that, if
possible, the families can remain together without
further threat to the children".

Regarding those required to report abuse/and or
neglect the act states:

K.S.A. 38-717..."Every teacher, school administrator or other employee of a school which such child is
attending...having reason to suspect that a child has
had injury or injuries inflicted upon him/her as a
result of physical or mental abuse or neglect shall

report...the matter promptly to the district court of
the county in which such...school is located....or
to the department of Social and Rehabilitation Services. Such report may be made orally, by telephoning
or otherwise and shall be followed by a written report if requested...Every such report when required
to be written shall contain, if known, the names and
addresses of the child and his/her care, the child's
age, the nature and the extent of the child's
injuries (incuding any evidence of previous injuries),
and other information that the maker of the report
believes might be helpful in establishing the cause
of the injuries and identity of the person or persons
allegedly responsible therefor."

Kansas State law protects the reporter from
liability in making a report of suspected child abuse
or neglect. The law reads:

K.S.A. 38-718....."Anyone participating without
malice in the making of an oral or written report....
shall have immunity from any liability, civil or
criminal, that might otherwise be incurred or imposed.

A final portion of the Kansas Child Protection
Act of importance to educators pertains to the issue
of confidenti-a-lity. The act states:

38-723...."All records and reports concerning
child abuse and neglect filed with the Department of
Social and Rehabilitation Services or a district court
are confidential and shall not be disclosed, and it
shall be a violation of the Kansas Child Protection
Act for any person....or other agency willfully or
knowingly to permit or encourage the unauthorized
dissemination of the contents of such records or
reports."

The Kansas Child Protection Act clearly identifies
educators among those mandated to report suspiscion of
child abuse or neglect. Original reporting statutes
required only medical personnel to report. The current
trend, however, is to identify a broad range of professionals in these statutes. As of 1979, forty-three
states and the District of Columbia specifically
mention educators in their laws. The other seven
states require any person suspecting child abuse or
neglect to make a report.[13]

In April 1980 the U.S. General Accounting Office
made a report to Congress on child abuse and neglect
which stated that professionals, including doctors
and teachers, frequently fail to report abuse and
neglect. The American Humane Association reported in
1978 that the school personnel account for only 11.6%
of reports made. Non-professionals, including
friends, neighbors, and relatives make up the largest
group of reporters at 38.4% however, after a report
has been made and a case is investigated, professionals, including school personnel, have been found to
play a much larger role in substantiating abuse and
neglect.[14]

A variety of reasons for the failure of teachers
to report are apparent. They include:[15]

(1) Lack of knowledge of the law or of indica-
    tors of child abuse.
(2) Fear of possible lawsuits or reprisals by
    parents.
(3) Reluctance to get involved.
(4) Belief that reporting would not really help
    and might even aggravate the situation.
(5) A previous bad experience when reporting.
(6) Building principals may discourage report-
    ing or not take teacher's concerns
    seriously.
(7) Lack of support from administrative staff.

Nevertheless, teachers are in a unique and
valuable position in terms of identifying children
who are abused or neglected. They see a child daily
over a period of time which offers them the opportunity to compare and contrast behavior and appearance over time. Most importantly, teachers are
legally and ethically obligated to act in the best
interests of the children under their care.[16]

Impact of Abuse and Neglect on Academic Achievement

The impact of abuse and neglect on academic
achievement has been well documented. A study performed by Utah State University in 1975 found that
twenty-seven percent of the one-hundred and thirty-
eight abused children they studied were subsequently
enrolled in special education classes. This is

contrasted with only eight percent of the general
school population placed in special education.
Exceptionalities represented in this study include
learning disabilities, emotionally disturbed, educable
mentally retarded, and those institutionalized.[17]
It is widely assumed that some children are exceptional prior to being abused or neglected and a portion
become exceptional as a result of abuse or neglect.

A 1976 study from the University of Southern
California found that abused children exhibit poor
school achievement, emotional withdrawl, poor peer
relationships, and agression toward adults and peers.
[18] It has also been found that abused children physically assault other children twice as often as non-
abused children. In this particular study, of all
children sampled, only abused children assaulted or
threatened to assault adults. Children who are abused
or neglected tend to be absent and tardy frequently
which directly affects academic functioning. They
may also be deficient in language skills, show poor
attention to task, and a consistent inability to
complete tasks. These skills are essential in maintaining good academic performance. Many abused
children are too preoccupied with survival functions
to develop these skills to the extent necessary to
excell in school.

Identification and Reporting of Abuse and Neglect

A variety of indicators of abuse or neglect are
evident in the classroom. These fall into four
categories-physical appearance, behavior, verbal
statements and academic performance. The prescence of
a single indicator is not necessarily indicative of
abuse or neglect. The duration, frequency, and
severity of indicators in a specific situation must
be considered. In the end, the judgment of the
individual determines whether a situation warrants a
report of suspected abuse or neglect.

Physical indicators which may be observed by a
teacher include:

    (a) Unexplained bruises, welts, lacerations, or
         burns. Thse on the back, face, or back of
         arms are particularly suspiscious. Also,

those forming regular patterns or reflect-
ing the shape of an article such as a belt
buckle.
(b) Poor hygiene.
(c) Inappropriate dress, for example, no coat
in cold weather or long sleeved shirts in
not weather.
(d) Unattended physical or medical needs.
(e) Difficulty walking or sitting.
(f) Behind peers in physical development.
Behavioral indicators may include:
(a) Chronic absenteeism or tardiness.
(b) Physical agression toward peers and/or
adults.
(c) Withdrawl, lethargy, or signs of depression.
(d) Sleeping in class.
(e) Fearful of adults.
(f) Coming early to school and remaining late
after school.
(g) Begging food.
(h) Run away, stealing, or other delinquent
behavior.
(i) Sophisticated or unusual sexual behavior.
(j) Infantile behavior (sucking, biting,
rocking).
(k) Poor peer relationships.
(l) Extreme emotional reactions.
Verbal statements made by a child can directly
or indirectly indicate abuse or neglect is taking
place. Statements may involve:
(a) Fear of going home or fear of parents.
(b) Reports of injuries inflicted by parents.
(c) Indications of hunger.
(d) Lack of supervision in the home.
(e) Reports of sexual assault.
(f) Continious physical complaints (with or
without apparent cause).
Academic indicators which may indicate abuse or
neglect include:
(a) A sudden change in level of performance.
(b) Poor language skills and/or speech disorders.
(c) Poor attention to task.
(d) Poor task completion.
(e) Inconsistent classroom performance.
Parent contact provide another sourch which may
suggest child abuse or neglect. The following
reactions are possible indicators:
(a) Blaming or belittling the child.
(b) Viewing the child as bad, evil, possessed,

89

etc.
(c) Lack of concern regarding child's behavior
     or academic functioning.
(d) Inability to find anything good or attract-
     ive in the child.
(e) Failure to keep appointments or respond to
     school requests.
(f) Bizzare or irrational behavior.[19]

When concerned about a particular child's situation but lacking specific information, a teacher
may want to keep a record of the child's behavior and
academic performance. Chart No. 1 suggests a format
teachers can use in helping them determine if a report of suspected chils abuse or neglect is warranted.
Charts Nos. 2 and 3 offer case examples using the
record keeping form. Situations or incidents which
are possible indicators of abuse or neglect are
briefly recorded and dated by the teacher. When
making a report, this allows the teacher to give
specific information rather than general impressions.

A suggested format for reporting the suspiscion
of child abuse or neglect is offered in chart No. 4.
Identifying information regarding the child, parents,
and siblings is given along with information regarding
the nature and extent of injuries, and any evidence
of previous injury. Identifying information of the
individual making the report is also listed. In
making a report this information is given orally or
in written form to the child protective services
worker at the local SRS office or to the local district court.

School Related Services

Schools may be involved with a child before
and/or after a report of suspected abuse is made.
Services may include special education placement;
support for parents in the form of parent education
programs, child development classes, counseling programs, or adult education programs; financial support
such as free or reduced lunches, and arrangeing for
the acquisition of glasses, hearing aids, clothing,
etc; and, finally, support for the child in the
regular classroom.

Classroom teachers can offer support by creating an atmosphere in which a child can experience competence and accomplishment. Positive school experiences enable a child to off-set feelings of inadequacy and self-doubt. Successful interactions with both adults and peers can help the abused child build a more positive self-image. Teachers can encourage parent involvement in a non-threatening, supportive manner. An angry note home from the school is more likely to endager the child and alienate the parent than to result in the parents cooperation. Whenever possible, it is important to stress the child's positive performance while suggesting wasy to improve any negative aspects. Teachers must be firm regarding standards of behavior for all students, including the abused or neglected child, and expectations of parents should be maintained but when it is necessary to take action teachers must strive to be positive and supportive.

Name of Child: _____

Date: <u>Situation or incident</u>

_____:

_____:

_____:

_____:

_____:

_____:

_____:

_____:

_____:

_____:

_____:

_____:

_____:

_____:

_____:

_____:

_____:

_____:

_____:

Case Example: Physical Abuse

Name of Child: Anne Brown 6 years. old

Date:

3-10-82 :   Observed bruise on upper arms that looked like hand prints.

3-19-82 :   Anne quiet in class. Not interacting with other children.

4-1-82 :   Cried in class when I yelled at another student.

4-4-82 :   Appears fearful of me and other adults. Never asks questions. Speaks only when spoken to.

4-10-82 :   Anne has been to the nurse several times this week but was not sick.

4-13-82 :   Played by herself at recess today. Rarely plays with other children.

4-17-82 :   Wore long sleeved shirt and pants today although it is warm outside Very inattentive in class. Did not complete her work which is unusual.

4-18-82 :   Observed numerous marks, scratches and bruises on back of Anne's legs and arms.

Chart No. 3

Case Example: Neglect

Name of Child: Mike Jones 10 yrs. old

Date:

9-21-81 : 30 minutes late to school

9-12-81 : Clothes soiled and torn. Hair dirty and uncombed. Ten minutes late.

9-13-81 : Unexcused absence.

9-16-81 : Fell asleep in class twice today.

9-17-81 : Not completing assignments.

9-19-81 : Complaining of hunger. Asking other kids for food.

9-20-81 : Hit and kicked another child at recess. Late again today. He is not turning in homework assignments.

9-24-81 : Called Mrs. Jones and scheduled a conference for 9-27-81. Mike is late again today.

9-27-81 : Mrs. Jones did not show up for scheduled appointment and did not call.

9-28-81 : Late to school. Agressive toward other children.

10-1-81 : (Pushing). Sent to principal's office. Called Mrs. Jones. Said she forgot our appointment. She is concerned about Mike's grades but says he is responsible for doing his homework and getting to school on time.

10-2-81 : Saw Mike on playground at 4:30 pm (school dismissed at 3:10 pm).

10-5-81 : Fell asleep in class today.

10-10-81 : Unexcused absence.

10-11-81 : Glasses have been broken for 3 weeks
and have not been repaired. Mike
unable to complete work and is
failing most subjects.

Options - Screening, contact school social
worker, contact protective services.

Suggested Format for Report of Suspected Child
Abuse and/or Neglect

Name of Child _____

Date of Birth _____

Address of Child _____

Name of Parents _____

Address of Parents _____

Telephone of Parents _____

Name(s) of Sibling _____

_____

_____

Nature and Extent of Child's Injuries: _____

_____

_____

_____

Evidence of Previous Injuries? _____

_____

_____

Name, Address and Telephone Number of Person Signing
This Report.

Name _____

Address _____

Telephone _____

(Signature) _____

References

1. Bourne, Richard and Eli Newberger. Critical Perspectives on Child Abuse. Toronto: Lexington Books, 1979.

2. Hare, Isadora. Child Protective Services: Standards for Service Delivery. National Conference on Social Welfare, May, 1980.

3. _____. "Reflections on Violence and Discipline," presented May 1-2, 1980, in a workshop MODE: Methods of Discipline in Education, Burlington, N.C., NASW: National Prof-Resource Center: Child Abuse and Neglect.

4. The Pass-along Problems of Parenting, Magazine Article by Mimi Swartz, Houston City Magazine. No date given. p. 247.

5. Stein, Theordore. Social Work Practice in Child Welfare. Englewood Cliffs: Prentice-Hall, Inc., 1981.

6. Ibid p. 63

7. Data Aspects of Child Protective Services. U.S. Dept. of Health and Human Services, September, 1980. A Report from the fourth National Conference on Data Aspects of Child Protective Services, Pub. No. 105-78-1101.

8. Wolkenstein, Alan. "Evolution of a Program for the Management of Child Abuse," Social Casework. May, 1976.

9. Child Protective Service: Intervention with the Sexually Victimized Child. NASW: National Professional Resource Center: Child Abuse and Neglect, September, 1980.

10. Conte, Jon R. and Lucy Berliner. "Sexual Abuse of Children: Implications for Practice," Social Casework. December, 1981, pp. 601- 606.

11. Hare, Isadora. "Legal Rights of Children: Child Abuse and Neglect and the School Social Worker", Paper presented at a National Invitational Workshop: School Social Work and the Law, Ann

Arbor, Michigan, May, 1980, p.1.

12. Kansas Child Protection Act, K.S.A. 38-716 to
    38-724, Wyandotte County Child Abuse Procedural
    Manual, Aug. 1979, pp. 32-37.

13. Hare, op. cit., p. 5.

14. Ibid p. 8.

15. Broadhurst, Diane D. "The Educator's Role in the
    Prevention and Treatment of Child Abuse and
    Neglect", National Center on Child Abuse and
    Neglect, U.S. Department of Health Education
    and Welfare, Aug. 1979. pp. 38-39.

16. Rowe, Jeanne. "How Teachers Can Help Victims of
    Child Abuse," Todays Education , April - May
    1981, p. 19.

17. Hare, op. cit., p.7

18. Rowe, op. cit., p. 19.

19. Broadhurst, op. cit. p. 16-20.

Section 5

Bias and Stereotyping

in School Materials

Because bias and sterotyping are frequently an unconscious practice, teachers-to-be, teachers, administrators and other school staff limit a students' opportunities without intending to do so. They simply continue biased practices because "that is the way it has always been done." However, in order to make significant changes in the school environment and build the school's capacity to provide instruction not limited by bias or stereotyping, educators need to make a conscious effort to learn new skills in identifying and compensating for bias.

Section 5 is designed to meet this challenge by: (1) helping educators understand what is meant by bias and stereotyping, how biased materials and instruction limit student's opportunities, and how educators can become effective agents for promoting equity; and (2) giving you skills in analyzing school materials for bias and stereotyping and developing action plan(s) to provide more equitable education for all students.

TEXTBOOKS AND INSTRUCTIONAL MATERIALS

One can easily become overwhelmed by the total number of instructional materials available for use in the classroom. The
National Education Association (1976), for example, lists 24 different kinds of instructional materials, including textbooks, films,
and newspapers. There are over 500,000 different materials available for classroom use.[1]

How important are instructional materials in the classroom?
Different studies have shown that 95% of all teaching time is spent
on the use of some type of instructional material.[2] Much of the
student's classroom time also is structured around printed material.

How much control as educator has over the instructional materials to be used in the classroom often depends on the school
district in which one teaches. The teacher may have some role in
selecting the textbook to be used in the classroom. Most often,
however, texts are assigned to teachers. Although some teachers
serve on a school district committee or state committee to select
textbooks for the area, most teachers have no role in the selection
process. Although it may seem that the teacher often does not
have much control over the textbooks to be used in the classroom,
it is an area in which the teacher can make some important decisions. In most cases, there is a great deal of latitude about
the kind of supplementary materials to be used. In most cases
there is a choice about how dependent the curriculum is on the
textbooks and materials that are assigned to the classroom. In
many schools, students are expected to be at a certain level of
academic competency by the time the school year ends. How the
teacher ensures that students learn the necessary concepts depends
on the teacher. As instructional decision makers, educators are
in influential positions.[3]

Many teachers have come to rely heavily on the textbook. A
textbook has been used often to determine the curriculum and sub-
sequent instructional strategies. Even for teachers who do not
rely heavily on the textbook to teach, it probably remains the
most important educational tool in classrooms of the past and
present. Other than the teacher and the chalkboard, the textbook
is probably the most standard item in all classrooms. How the
teacher uses textbooks and other instructional materials is extremely important in providing a multicultural perspective.

One of the problems in depending so heavily on the textbook
for classroom instruction is that many educators never suspect
the validity of its contents. We read the information as if it
were unquestionalbly accurate and usually are not encouraged to
question its validity. Consequently, it is difficult to begin

reading critically for multicultural content and sensitivity. To provide a multicultural perspective, educators first need to examine critically the materials used in the classroom. We must be able to recognize the biases that often exist in such materials [4] and develop instructional strategies to counteract those biases.

Sadker and Sadker[5] identified six forms of bias that are useful in examining classroom materials. These biases include (1) invisibility, (2) stereotyping, (3) selectivity and imbalance, (4) unreality, (5) fragmentation and isolation, and (6) language.

INVISIBILITY

Means that certain groups are underrepresented in materials. This omission implies that these groups have less value, importance, and significance in our society. Invisibility in instructional materials occurs most frequently for women, minority groups, handicapped individuals, and older persons.

Materials can be examined for invisibility simply by counting the number of different groups represented in illustrations, in various occupations, in biographies, or as main characters. For example, this technique was used by researchers who analyzed 134 readers and found the following ratios:[6]

* Boy-centered stories to girl-centered stories   7:2
* Male illustrations to female illustrations   2:1
* Male occupations to female occupations   3:1
* Male biographies to female biographies   2:1

Another study of science, math, reading, spelling and social studies textbooks revealed that only 31% of all illustrations included girls and women and that the percentage of females decreased as the grade level increased. This same pattern was found for illustrations of minority persons. The most invisible member of school texts was the minority female.[7]

ADDITIONAL FACTORS TO CONSIDER:

Do the materials include contributions and a variety of roles of both men and women of different ages, physical abilities and ethnic groups?

Are a variety of socioeconomic levels and settings (urban, rural, suburban) included?

Is diversity in terms of religion, cultures and family structure included?

It is important that visual images accurately depict physical images, life styles, cultural traditions and surroundings when portraying persons from different racial/ethnic backgrounds. It is not enough to simply change skin color or names.

STEREOTYPING

By assigning traditional and rigid roles or attributes to a group, instructional materials stereotype and limit the abilities and potential of that group. Not only are careers stereotyped, but so to- are intellectual abilities, personality characteristics, physical appearance, social status and domestic roles. Stereotyping denies students a knowledge of the diversity, complexity, and variation of any group of individuals.

THE COMPLEXITY OF STEREOTYPING:

MY DEFINITION: _____

_____

_____

_____

Two schools of thought in regard to stereotypes and stereotyping:
1. ANY and ALL stereotypes are incorrect, or
2. On the contrary.... what about GROUP NORMS ?

What is your position concerning these two thoughts/beliefs?

_____

_____

_____

_____

_____

_____

Questions to consider:

A. Stereotyped thinking is <u>not</u> always undesirable, harmful or stupid. Agree _____ Disagree _____ Provide an example.

_____

_____

_____

_____

B. Generalizations are valid if they are based on solid data.
Agree _____ Disagree _____ Provide an example.

_____

_____

_____

_____

C. Some stereotypes express favorable attitudes. Agree _____
Disagree _____ Provide an example:

_____

_____

_____

_____

D. Stereotypes are difficult to refute. Agree _____ Disagree _____
Why ? _____

_____

_____

_____

E. Stereotypes are <u>not</u> identical with prejudice. Agree _____
Disagree _____ Why: _____

_____

ADDITIONAL FACTORS TO CONSIDER WHEN EXAMINING MATERIALS FOR
STEREOTYPES AND STEREOTYPING:

* Do men and women, boys and girls, show a wide variety of emotions?

* Are both sexes involved in active and passive activities, in-
dooors and outdoors?

* Do visual depictions make clearly apparent the differences in
appearance within a group as well as between groups?

* Does the plot/ story line exaggerate the exoticism or mysticism
of the various ethnic groups? For example customs/ festivals.

* Are older people shown in active as well as passive roles?

* Is old age and aging usually equated with death?

* Are disabled persons usually portrayed as members of problem
ridden families?

* Do represenatives from previously excluded groups have to have
a super hero(es) characteristics?

* Do members of the aforementioned categories fill both support
and leadership roles?

SELECTIVITY AND IMBALANCE

Occurs when issues and situations are interpreted from only
one perspective, usually the perspective of the majority group.
Many issues, situations, and events described in textbooks are
complex and can be viewed from a variety of viewpoints/ or perspectives. Often, only one perspective is presented. For example,
the relationships between the U.S. government and the American
Indians are usually examined only from the government's perspective
in terms of treaties and protection. An American Indian perspective would also examine broken treaties and the appropriation
of native lands. This is an example of bias through selectivity
and imbalance.

WHAT CAN I DO ABOUT THIS SITUATION?

As a prospective classroom teacher, we must be conscious of
what textbooks and curriculum materials in general present. Although the materials you may use may indeed be limited in their
viewpoints, your sensitivity and understanding can then provide
further research, discussion by your students to look at the issue
or situation from another point of view. It is not necessary that

each and every situation or event be examined with this indepth
scrutiny, but once students become aware and condition to look
at situations/ issues from a variety of perspectives - then the
role of the classroom teacher can become one of facilitator in
discussing the various options that present themselves.

UNREALITY

Textbooks frequently present an unrealistic portrayal of our
history and contemporary life experiences. Controversial topics
are glossed over, and discussions of discrimination and prejudice
are avoided. When sensitive and unpleasant issues, such as racism,
sexism, prejudice, discrimination, intergroup conflict, divorce
and death are not included in instructional materials, students
are not provided guidance in handling such complex issues. Contemporary problems faced by the hanidcapped or aged are often dis-
guised or simply not included. American Indians, in discussions
or illustrations, are often pictured in historical context rather
than a contemporary image. Most materials do not consider sex
bias and race bias that exist in employment practices and in salary
schedules. The avoided issues include those that many students
will have to face in the near future. This unrealistic coverage
denies/prohibits students the information needed to recognize,
understand, and perhaps someday conquer that problems that plague
our society.[8]

How would you respond to the concern that "textbook censorship" is an area that needs the community, parent(s) and teachers
close scrutiny. Agree _____ Disagree _____

Does this UNREALITY section in examining materials fall into
this category - of censorship ? Explain:

_____

_____

_____

_____

_____

FRAGMENTATION AND ISOLATION

Is a popular method in which many publishers include some of
the ethnic minority groups, women etc. in their instructional
materials. Issues, contributions, and information that we have

105

previously discussed as being relevant is typically separated from the regular text and discussed in a "section" or "chapter" of their own. This "add-on" approach is easier to accomplish than trying to integrate the information throughout the text. There is nothing wrong with having some information separate from the regular text if it is not the only place students read about members of a specific group. The isolation of this information often has negative connotations or messages for students. This approach suggests that the experiences and contributions of these groups are merely an interesting diversion and not an integral part of historical and contemporary developments. Society is pluralistic, and it is important that instructional materials and textbooks reflect this diversity as a part of the total text rather than discussing particular groups in a separate section or as an "add-on."

Do you think it is possible for publishers and textbook authors to fully integrate materials that would "get away" from the add-on approach frequently found today? _____yes _____no

Is there a particular level or subject area that would be more able to accomplish full integration? _____ yes _____no

Explain your answer and provide an example: _____

_____

_____

_____

_____

On the other hand, is there a particular level or subject area that would be more difficult to achieve an integrated approach in their curricular materials? _____ yes _____no

Explain you answer and provide an example: _____

_____

_____

_____

_____

_____

LANGUAGE

In the examination of curricular materials in the area of language usage, there are several questions one should atleast consider.

* Is the language and terminology used up-to-date?

* Is the language void of derogatory words or phrases?

* Are the terms used to refer to an individual or group so BROAD they are inaccurate or non-descript? For example: Indian vs. American Indian or Native American vs. Dakota.

* Is parallel language used when describing the sexes? For example: men - women, ladies - gentlemen, boys - girls, rather than men - ladies, or men - girls.

* Others to add:

*

LOOKING AT ALTERNATIVES

Often our own language that we use daily may be the first place to start in "sensitizing" ourselves to the concepts of providing equitable and fair treatment to all. As a prosective classroom teacher, this is one area in which are verbal behavior and communication skills may indeed send a message to our students. What would you consider an appropriate and more meaningful alternative(s) to the common word or phrases used below?

Common terminology	My Alternative(s)
Chairman	_____
Fireman	_____
Culturally Deprived	_____
"OK! Let's all sit Indian Style."	_____

Common Terminology	My Alternative(s)
She's a Career Girl	_____
Policeman	_____
Oh! Yeah, Sarah is crippled.	_____
Gosh! I'll bet I am on their Black List.	_____
Dear Gentleman/ Dear Sir:	_____
Congressman	_____
Mailman	_____
Old People	_____
Salesman	_____
Oh! You Indian Giver!	_____
Oh! Molly. That's not very Lady-like.	_____
I am going to try and "Jew them down" first.	_____
No, I don't agree, I think Randy is retarded.	_____
Businessman	_____
Come on Michael, don't be a sissy!	_____
Your all acting like a bunch of wild Indians!	_____

Now add to the list:

_____	_____
_____	_____
_____	_____

EVALUATING MATERIALS

There are numerous guidelines, charts and forms for the evaluation of curriculum materials in the field of education today. Every educational organization, school district and scholarly publication, has at one time or another, proposed their method for evaluating materials. My point, is that with a little bit of effort on your part – you can put your hands on various examples of these guidelines. In other words, the problem hasn't been one of the lack of direction, but one of "how to go about it systematically." Evaluating materials, put quite simply, is not an easy task. It becomes even more confusing for the person who hasn't worked with materials in a classroom setting and had the day-to-day exerience of teaching.

That is not to offer an excuse to you, but to assure you that with experience in the classroom coming, you can begin to prepare yourself by looking over some materials and gain some practical in-sight into what to "look for" in evaluating materials. We need to get away from the mentality that if it's in a book – it must be O.K. As we will learn along the way, there are a great amount of curriculum materials that are very well done, but at the same time there are a great amount of materials that are very weak in the area(s) that we are concerned with. So, if we can image a continum as the one described below – this really is the diversity that we can find in the materials used in schools today.

EFFORTS IN PROVIDING EQUITABLE TREATMENT

X	X	X	X
NONE	BRIEF MENTION	SOME EVIDENCE	OVERALL INTEGRATION

Your task is to find a book(s) in your subject area and level from two distinct periods of time. For example, one book published in 1965 and the other from 1980. It will provide you an example of what was available several years ago and what is being used today. In some cases, depending upon level and subject area, you will see distinct changes in content and illustrations offered from the two periods of time. And, some of you will see a very little amount of effort during this period of transition from the "melting pot" concept to the pluralistic movement in materials we are all concerned with.

The following chart and form to "fill-out" should be used to record your findings. It is hoped that this experience will increase our skill in "looking at" materials for what they offer and what they don't.

THE REPORT OF "MULTICULTURAL" INPUT

LEVEL I	NO MULTICULTURAL INPUT
LEVEL II	BRIEF MENTION OF MULTICULTURAL CONCEPTS MINIMAL SENSITIZING ADD-ON SECTIONS
LEVEL III	SOME INTEGRATION DEVELOPMENT OF EXAMPLES PROVIDED SOME SENSITIZING TO ISSUES
LEVEL IV	OVERALL INTEGRATION IN-DEPTH DEVELOPMENT ALTERNATIVE PROVIDED CHALLENGES AND SENSITIZES

EVALUATING CURRICULUM MATERIALS

Name of Evaluator: _____

Title: _____

Publisher: _____

Date of Publication: (Dated Material) _____

Most Appropriate Level: _____ Elementary

_____ Middle Level

_____ Secondary

_____ Post-Secondary

PERTINENT ISSUES / AREAS TO CONSIDER

RATE THE LEVEL OF INPUT 1 2 3 4	(Ethnicity, sex, age, exceptional groups) *You may wish to add or delete, but this should be the basis of our evaluation*
	Diversity of Illustrations offered (integrated)
	Up-to-date terminology
	Unbiased Language
	Realistic Portrayls (Non-Stereotypical)
	Wide Variety of Perspective Offered
	Content is well integrated throughout the material (no evidence of add-on approach)
	Total Score (24 points possible)

_____ I would highly recommend this material (22-24 pts)

_____ I would consider this material above average (19-21 pts)

_____ I would consider this material average (16-18 pts)

_____ I would consider this material below average (13-15 pts)

_____ I would not recommend this material (12 and below)

A. Why did you rate the material as you did? Explain your score.

_____

_____

_____

_____

_____

_____

B. Identify specific examples to support your score. (Page numbers, examples, sample statements etc.)

_____

_____

_____

_____

_____

_____

_____

C. Additional Comments/ Suggestions you wish to make concerning this particular material.

_____

_____

EVALUATING CURRICULUM MATERIALS

Name of Evaluator: _____

Title: _____

Publisher: _____

Date of Publication: (Recent Material) _____

Most Appropriate Level: _____ Elementary

_____ Middle Level

_____ Secondary

_____ Post-Secondary

PERTINENT ISSUES / AREAS TO CONSIDER

RATE THE LEVEL OF INPUT				(Ethnicity, sex, age, exceptional groups) *You may wish to add or delete, but this should be the basis of our evaluation*
1	2	3	4	
				Diversity of Illustrations offered (integrated)
				Up-to-date terminology
				Unbiased Language
				Realistic Portrayls (Non-Stereotypical)
				Wide Variety of Perspective Offered
				Content is well integrated throughout the material (no evidence of add-on approach)
				Total Score (24 points possible)

_____ I would highly recommend this material (22-24 pts)

_____ I would consider this material above average (19-21 pts)

_____ I would consider this material average (16-18 pts)

_____ I would consider this material below average (13-15 pts)

_____ I would not recommend this material (12 and below)

A. Why did you rate the material as you did? Explain your score.

_____

_____

_____

_____

_____

_____

B. Identify specific examples to support your score. (Page numbers, examples, sample statements etc.)

_____

_____

_____

_____

_____

_____

C. Additional Comments/ Suggestions you wish to make concerning this particular material.

_____

_____

EXAMINING THE INFORMAL CURRICULUM

Schools do not monopolize multicultural education nor will they do so in the future, even if they so wish. Why? Because all students, all people, coninuously receive a multicultural education - both positive and negative - outside schools. Aware of it or not, we are all students of this informal curriculum.

What is the informal curriculum? It is that massive, ongoing, informal curriculum of family, peer groups, neighborhoods, churches, organizations, occupations, mass media, and other "socializing" forces that "educate" all of us throughout our lives.[10]

This informal curriculum comprises at least four components: (1) home, peer group(s), and neighborhood; (2) organizations and institutions; (3) the media; and (4) personal contacts with ethnic experiences. For each person, some aspects of that curriculum work positively to increase sensitivity to and understanding about different groups. For each person, other aspects have negative impact through spreading distortions, building stereotypes, or increasing prejudice.

The media - television, motion pictures, radio, newspapers, and magazines - rank among the most powerful and pervasive aspects of the informal curriculum.[11]

For example, let us look at television. The first point to be made about televsion and school is to observe that each of them is a curriculum. The first task of a curriculum is to engage the attention of its students for a certain period of time. Thus there are two questions to be addressed: How much time? How to get their attention? If we assume a child will go to school for 13 years - say, starting in kindergarten and ending with high school - a typical American child will be in the presence of a school curriculum 2,340 days, or about 11,500 hours. There are only two activities that occupy more of a youngster's time during those years: sleeeping and atteding to television.[12]

Studies of TV viewing are far from definitive, but a fair estimate is that from age 5 to 18 an American child watches TV for approximately 15,000 hours. That is 30% more time than he/she is engaged in school, a very significant difference. If we add to the 15,000 hours of TV viewing the time occupied by radio and record listening, video games, movie-going, we come up with a figure very close to 20,000 hours of exposure to an electronic media curriculum- almost double the amount of time spent in school.

WHAT MESSAGES DO WE GET FROM THE INFORMAL CURRICULUM ?

Just as we have to learn how to examine curriculum materials, it is also vital that we learn how to examine the social forces that obviously have a great impact on our education. The informal curriculum that I have briefly mentioned is real, it will not go away and obviously there are many things we would like to have improved with it. However, as a classroom teacher, one can take advantage of this informal curriculum and use it as a learning tool with you students. If it indeed is a fact that we all spend more time within this informal curriculum, why not use it as an asset in our "formal" curriculum?

But, first we must become aware ourselves of the messages that are continually being given to us in this "informal" setting. Given the focus and concern of providing a more equitable perspective within our "formal" curriculum, it would be beneficial to learn and examine the messages that are supporting this notion through the "informal" curriculum. Also, those messages which we may feel are counter productive to what we endorse in the formal setting.

QUESTIONS TO CONSIDER IN EXAMINING THE MESSAGES GIVEN TO US:

Again, the "informal" curriculum covers a broad range of factors, i.e., family, neighborhoods, peer groups to media. For this particular exercise, let us look at the different forms of media that are in our society and get a "feel" for the messages coming from that one aspect of the "informal" education we all receive.

(Television, motion pictures, radio, newspapers and magazines)

* Is there an attempt to provide a pluralistic portrayal in the media?

* Is there a common "trend" when certain groups of people are portrayed through the media. For example, the elderly, women.

* Is there a "balance" with the representation given through the media?

* Are they void of stereotypes and un-biased language?

* Is there a slanted perspective given? (Radio, newspapers, magazines)

* Overall, what are the messages saying in regard to providing or endorsing a multicultural perspective?

116

EVALUATING THE INFORMAL CURRICULUM

(PRINTED MEDIA)

Name of Evaluator: _____

Type of Media: _____ magazine _____ newspaper
(Please check)
              _____ article _____ advertisement

Circle appropriate items: daily   Sunday   weekly   monthly

neighborhood   local   regional   national   other _____

Date of Publication: _____

Title: (of article, advertisement evaluated) _____

_____

_____

****

Describe the story, event or product: _____

_____

_____

_____

Primary Charcter(s) (Describe roles portrayed) _____

_____

_____

_____

Secondary Character(s) (Describe roles portrayed) _____

_____

_____

_____

Is there are ethnic minority representation? _____ yes _____ no

If so, who are they ? _____

_____

_____

Did they portray a primary character or secondary character?

_____

_____

Is there any representation from the elderly, exceptional populations, women/men given? _____ yes _____ no

If so, who are they? _____

_____

_____

Did they portray a primary character or secondary character?

_____

_____

In looking at the last two questions on this page, are there any stereotypical images or portrayals given to those particular groups?

_____ yes _____ no Explain: _____

_____

_____

_____

If you had the opportunity to re-write, re-design the printed media that you have just evaluated, how would you change it? Or would you be satisfied the way it is now?

_____

_____

EVALUATING THE INFORMAL CURRICULUM

(VISUAL MEDIA)

Name of Evaluator: _____

Type of Media:
(Please Check) _____ television _____ movie

_____ other

Date of Evaluation: _____

Title: (of advertisement, program etc.) _____

_____

_____

_____

_____

****

Describe the story, event or product: _____

_____

_____

_____

_____

Primary Character(s) (Describe roles portrayed) _____

_____

_____

_____

Secondary Character(s) (Describe roles portrayed) _____

_____

_____

Was there any ethnic minority representation? _____ yes ___ no

Is so, who are they ? _____

_____

_____

Did they portray a primary character(s) or secondary character(s)?

_____

_____

Was there any representation from the elderly, exceptional populations, women/men given? _____ yes _____ no

If so, who are they? _____

_____

_____

Did they portray a primary character(s) or secondary character(s)?

_____

_____

In looking at the last two questions on this page, are there any stereotypical images or portrayals given to those particular groups? _____ yes _____ no Explain: _____

_____

_____

_____

If you had the opportunity to re-write, re-design the visual media that you have just evaluated, how would you change it? Or would you be satisfied the way it was done?

_____

_____

_____

_____

References

1. National Education Association. <u>Instructional Materials:
Selection and Purchase.</u> Washington, D.C.: The Association,
1976.

2. EPIE Institute. <u>Report on a national study of the nature
and the quality of instructional materials most used by
teachers and learners.</u> New York: The Institute, 1977.

3. Gollnick, D.M., Sadker, M.P. and Sadker, D.M. <u>Beyond the
Dick and Jane Syndrome: Confronting sex bias in instructional materials.</u> In M.P. Sadker and D.M. Sadker (Eds.),
<u>Sex equity handbook for schools.</u> New York: Longman, 1982.

4. Chinn, Phillip C., and Gollnick, D.M., <u>Multicultural
Education in a Pluralistic Society.</u> The C.V. Mosby Co.,
St. Louis, Missouri. 1983.

5. Sadker, M., and Sadker, D. The teacher educator's role.
In S. McCune and M. Matthews (Eds.), <u>Implementing Title IX
and attaining sex equality; A workshop package for post-
secondary educators.</u> Washington, D.C.: U.S. Government
Printing Office, 1978.

6. Women on Words and Images. <u>Dick and Jane as Victims: Sex
Stereotyping in children's readers.</u> Princeton, N.J. 1975.

7. Weitzman, L.J., and Rizzo, D. <u>Biased Textbooks: A research
perspective.</u> Washington, D.C.: Resource Center on Sex
Roles in Education, 1974.

8. Ibid. Sadker, M., and Sadker, D. 1978.

9. Ibid, Chinn, Phillip C., Gollnick, D.M. 1983

10. Cortes, Carlos,E., <u>The Role of Media in Multicultural Education,</u> Viewpoints in Teaching and Learning. 56 (Winter
1980)

11. Ibid, Cortes.

12. Postman, Neil. "<u>The First Curriculum: Comparing School and
Television.</u>" Phi Delta Kappan. 61: 163-168 November 1979.

121

What Can You Do About

Biased Materials?

Individual awareness and sensitivity of providing equity in
textbooks and instructional materials is an important FIRST step
in changing biased materials and their impact on all of us. Each
of us has a responsibility for using our awareness to bring about
some changes and SUPPORT others who are working in this area.

As a prospective classroom teacher, or a teacher today, I would:

* Look for and learn to recognize bias that may be found in curricular materials. (textbooks, library books, magazines, television
programs etc.)

* "Level" with the students in your classroom. Point out bias or
stereotypical portrayals in the curriculum materials. Help them
learn to identify sources of bias and important omissions in the
materials.

* Develop classroom activities around identifying bias found in
television, textbooks, movies, library books, magazines etc.

* Identify or develop supplementary materials which can help
"correct" some of the representation found in many of the materials.

* Design student research projects. These could include a study of
their own textbook materials or their identification of supplementary materials. (This would vary according to level(s)).

* Assign student research,(papers, themes, term papers) or other
activities on topics or persons NOT usually covered in textbooks or
materials.

* Ask students to rewrite materials, write their own materials on
subjects omitted from the textbook, or rewrite the material from
another person's point of view.

* Use bulletin boards, posters, pictures, magazines, and other materials to expose students to information commonly excluded from
traditional materials.

* Develop an ongoing collection of "unbiased" reading materials for
students. Identify books that students may be encouraged to seek

out in their personal reading.

* Request and use funds available for instructional materials in building supplementary materials resources for your classroom use of school wide use.

* Conduct a study and periodic review of the bias found in the text-books and materials used in your classroom or in the school.

* Meet with school media specialists, librarians and ask them to assist teachers and administrators in the identification of unbiased materials. Urge them to order and provide up-to-date resources that are becoming available daily.

* Organize a central file in your school building or district of supplementary materials, curriculum outlines, or other resources that you have used for identifying bias and supplenting the curriculum.

* Develop a "YELLOW PAGES" of resources for multicultural education would be helpful to faculty; this might include a list of speakers, resource persons in the community, ethnic group organizations, social service agencies, and places for good out-of-class learning experiences within the community.

* Identify non-traditional publishing firms, alternative presses, and other groups developing materials in this area. Distribute this information to all staff. (Suggested list in Section 6).

* Publicize studies, workshops and other efforts to improve materials or reduce the impact of biased materials.

YOUR PERSONAL RESPONSE TO EQUITY

As a prospective classroom teacher, what could I be doing along the way to best prepare myself to teach with a multicultural perspective?

* During my own personal research efforts in my teacher training program, a multicultural perspective will always at least be given strong consideration.

* Evaluate more critically what I am presently doing and using in my course(s) and subject area responsibilities.

* Look more carefully in my own school, university, or city library for equitable materials to assist my teaching area(s).

123

* Start keeping an original file (personal) that identifies those aids, guidelines, materials, visuals, etc. that I would like to have access to in my first teaching assignment.

* When assigned the task of "designing" or "developing" lesson plans in my subject area(s), they will be unbiased and endorse a multicultural perspective.

* When taking courses in the content area, to address the question if this is really preparing me in a perspective that will assist me in my teaching? That is, is the "content" presented in a multicultural perspective? If not, why isn't it? It's your responsibility to bring this to the attention of the instructor. If we don't become advocates for change, then we could be part of the problem!

* Don't get caught up in a "save the world" crusade. Be <u>realistic</u> and <u>honest</u> with yourself.

* Don't assume the posture, that multicultural education isn't really my area. It's being "taken care of" by someone else.

* Don't be afraid to take a risk! <u>Use</u> and <u>practice</u> a variety of teaching styles and materials. <u>Be able to learn along with your classmates and future students.</u>

* Don't expect to find the "packaged deal" that has everything you'll – need to teach your subject area(s) with a multicultural perspective. <u>It doesn't exist!</u>

‡ We must begin to learn through our training that we can not and should not depend solely on "the" textbook as the primary means of teaching our future students. Variety is the spice of life and a well-balanced variety of resources at your finger-tips will only provide your future students the most meaningful educational experience we all are striving to provide.

*NOTE: Your overall personal response to the concept of providing an equitable educational experience for your students   may begin to tell you something about your own attitude, beliefs and behaviors that you have concerning this area. Your personal postion or "frame of reference" often will determine your COMMITMENT and role that you will play in the effort that it requires to the concept. As a prospective classroom teacher, you really need to stop and determine if you can personally and educationally agree with the concept. If you can't agree, then you must go back and examine those stumbling blocks before you attempt to organize, plan and implement this concept within your teaching philosophy. It may help to determine if your disagreement is based on personal attitudes or a concern for your students.

Section 6:

Resources

Introduction

Section 6 is a compilation of resources available to all of us concerned with multicultural education. Often, teachers and administrators ask me, "Where do I get materials to begin?" There are several sources that a person can contact for materials, or simply be placed on a mailing list. The resources provided in this book are from a variety of sources. They include:

1)   An Introductory Bibliography for Multicultural Education
2)   Free and Inexpensive Materials for Teaching
3)   Libraries - "Selected Outstanding Ethnic Programs"
4)   Periodical Resources
5)   Organizational Resources

MULTICULTURAL EDUCATION

BASIC REFERENCES

AACTE-Multicultural Teacher Education, 4 Volumes (Case studies, resources, guidelines, and preparatory), 1980.

A Better Chance To Learn: Bilingual-Bicultural Education. United States Commission on Civil Rights Clearinghouse, Publication 51, May, 1975.

Banks, James A. "Multiethnic Education: Theory and Practice." Boston: Allyn and Bacon, 1981.

Banks, James A. Teaching Strategies for Ethnic Studies. Boston: Allyn and Bacon, 1975.

Banks, James (Editor). Education in the 80's: Multiethnic Education. National Education Association, Washington, D.C., 1981.

Banks, James et.al. "Curriculum Guidelines for Multiethnic Education." Washington, D.C., National Council for the Social Studies, 1976.

Banks, James A., Joyce, William W. Teaching Social Studies to Culturally Different Children. Addison-Wesley Publishing Company: Reading, Mass., 1971.

Baptise, H. Prentice, Jr. "Multicultural Education: A Synopsis." Washington, D.C., University Press of America, 1976.

Chase, Josephine, Prath, Linda. Multicultural Spoken Here. Goodyear Publishing Co., 1979.

Colangelo, Nicholas. Multicultural/Non-sexist Education. Kendal/Hunt Publishing Co., 1979.

Cortes, Carlos E., et.al. "Understanding You and Them: Tips for Teaching About Ethnicity." Boulder, Colorado. Social Science Education Consortium, 1976.

Cross, Delores E., et.al. Teaching in a Multicultural Society: Perspectives and Professional Strategies. New York: Macmillian, 1977.

Daniels, Roger, Kitano, Harry H.L. American Racism: Exploration of the Natural of Prejudice. Prentice-Hall, Inc. 1970.

Ehlers, Henry. "Crucial Issues in Education." Holt, Rinehart, and Winston, 7th Edition, New York, 1981.

Epps, Edgar G. Cultural Pluralism. McCutchan Publishing Corporation: Berkeley, 1974.

Fair-Textbooks--A Resource Guide. United States Commission on Civil Rights, Clearinghouse Publication 61, Washington, D.C., December, 1979.

Fishman, Joshua A. Bilingual Education, An International Sociological Perspective. Newbury House Publishers, Inc. 1976.

Glazer, Nathan, Moynihan, Daniel (eds.) Ethnicity: Theory and Experience. Cambridge, Mass: Harvard University Press, 1975.

Gold, Grant, Risilin (eds.) In Praise of Diversity: A Resource Book for Multicultural Education. Teacher Corps: Washington, D.C., 1977.

Gomez, David F. Somos Chicanos: Strangers in Our Own Land. Beacon Press: Boston, 1973.

Goodman, Mary Ellen. Race Awareness in Young Children. Collier MacMillan Publishing Co., 1964.

Gordon, Milton. Assimilation in American Life: The Role of Race, Religion, and National Origins. New York: Oxford University Press, 1964.

Grant, Carl. In Praise of Diversity--A Resource Book for Multicultural Education. Teacher Corps, 1977.

Grant, Carl A. (ed.) Multicultural Education: Commitments, Issues, and Applications. ASCD, 1977.

Grant, Gloria. In Praise of Diversity--Multicultural Classroom Applications. Teacher Corps, 1977.

Greeley, Andrew. Ethnicity in the United States: A Preliminary Reconnaissance. New York: John Wiley & Sons, 1974.

Grove, Cornelius Lee. Communications Across Cultures: A Report on Cross-Cultural Research. Washington, D.C., National Education Association, 1976.

Hartman, Edward G. The Movement to Americanize the Immigrant. New York: Columbia Univeristy Press, 1948.

Hirsch, Carl S. Racism in America. McDougal, Littell & Co., 1974.

Hughes, Helen MacGill. Racial and Ethnic Relations. Allyn and Bacon, Inc., 1976.

Hunter, William A. (ed.) Multicultural Education through Competency Based Teacher Education. American Association of Colleges for Teacher Education, 1974.

Jones, James M. Prejudice and Racism. Addison-Wesley Publishing Co., 1972.

Jones, Reginald. L. (ed.) Mainstreaming and the Minority Child. Leadership Training Institute, 1976.

King, Edith. Teaching Ethnic Awareness--Methods and Materials for the Elementary School. Goodyear Publishing Co., Inc. Santa Monica, California, 1980.

Kitano, Harry L.H. Race Relations. Prentice-Hall, Sociology Series, 1974.

Klassen, Gollnick (eds.) Pluralism and the American Teacher, Issues and Case Studies. AAETE, 1977.

Knowles, Louis L., Prewitt, Kenneth. Institutional Racism in America. Prentice-Hall, Inc., 1969.

Levin, Jack. The Functions of Prejudice. New York: Harper and Row, 1975.

Linskie, Rosella and Rosenberg, Howard. A Handbook for Multicultural Studies in Elementary Schools. Book I. R&E Research Associates, 1978.

Morris, Lee (Editor). Extracting Learning Styles from Social/ Cultural Diversity--A Study of Five American Minorities. Southwest Teacher Corps Network, 1978.

Noar, Gertrude. "The Teacher and Integration." Rev. Ed. Washington, D.C., National Education Association, 1974.

Otero, George and Smith, Gary. Teaching About Cultural Awareness, Center for Teaching International Relations, University of Denver, Vol. II, 1977.

Prejudice and Discrimination: Challenges of Our Time. Allyn and Bacon, 1973.

Ramirex, Manuel, and Castaneds, Alfredo. Cultural Democracy, Bicognitive Development, and Education. Academic Press, 1974.

Rist, Ray. The Urban School: A Factory for Failure. The MIT Press, 1973.

Rodriguez, Fred. "Mainstreaming a Multicultural Concept into Special Education - Guidelines for Teacher Trainers." University of Kansas, School of Education, 1980.

Rodriguez, Fred. The Treatment of Different Languages in the United States: A Brief Historical Survey. Lucas Brother Publishers, 1979.

Rose, Peter I. They and We: Racial and Ethnic Relations in the United States, 2nd ed. New York: Random House, 1974.

Schneider, Susan Gilbert. Revolution, Reaction or Reform: The 1974 Bilingual Ed. Act. L.A. Publishing Company, 1976.

Smith, Brewster M., Piliavin, June A. The Schools and Prejudice: Findings. Frederich A. Praeger, Inc., 1969.

Stent, Hazard, Rivilin (eds.) Cultural Pluralism: A Mandate for Change, Appleton-Century Crofts, 1973.

"The Condition of Education for Hispanic Americans." National Center for Educational Statistics, U.S. Government Printing Office, Washington, D.C., 20402, February, 1980. 268 pps.

Tiedt, Iris and Tiedt, Pamela. Multicultural Teaching--A Handbook of Activities, Information and Resources. Allyn and Bacon, 1979.

Tyack, David B. The One Best System: A History of American Urban Education. 1974.

Van den Berghe, Pierre L. Race and Racism: A Comparative Perspective, New York: John Wiley & Sons, 1967.

Vander Zanden, James W. American Minority Relations, 3rd ed. New York: Ronald Press, 1972.

Wahley, Nita B. Human Relations: Current Trends in School Policies and Practices. National School Public Relations Association, 1972.

Weinberg, Meyer. A Chance to Learn: A History of Race and Education in the United States. Cambridge University Press, 1977.

Wilkerson, Doxey (ed.) "Educating All Our Children." Mediax, Inc., 21 Charles St., Westport, Conn., 06880. 1979. 173 pps.

FREE AND INEXPENSIVE MATERIALS FOR TEACHING

Free and Inexpensive Aids

Cooperative Estension Service, Box U-35, The University of Connecticut, Storrs, CT 06268. Mexican Foods and Traditions (25¢).

Delmonte Teaching Aids, Box 4007, Clinton, IA 52732. The Big Four Daily Countdown (basic foods). Sonsuma Diariamente Los Cuatro Alimentos Basicos.

Frito-Lay Tower, Dallas, TX 75235. Tasty Recipes from Frito-Lay, Inc.

Multicultural Modules, Contemporary Press, Box 1524, San Jose, CA 95109. Chinese Americans ($1.50), Spanish-speaking American ($1.50), Black American ($1.50).

National Dairy Council, Chicago, IL 60606. Una Guia Para Comer Bieh - Chart.

Texas Education Agency, 201 East 11th St., Austin, TX 78701. El Corrido de Gregorio Cortez. (Send blank tape, cassette size).

Free and Inexpensive Mateials

American Library Association, 50 East Huron St., Chicago, IL 60611. American Indians: A Bibliography of Sources, a list of many recent materials, (50¢).

_____ . Children's Books of International Interest Printed In U.S.A., a selective 1sst, (free).

Asia Society, 112 East 64th St., New York, NY 10021. Asia: A Guide to Basic Books, a list of basic books on Asia (50¢).

Baker, Augusta. Office of Children's Services, New York Public Library, 8 East 40th St., New York, NY 10016. The Black Experience in Children's Books, a revision that includes 400 titles, (50¢).

California Library Association, 1741 Solano Ave., Berkeley, CA 94707. American Negro in Contemporary Society, an annotated list of 121 titles, (free).

Centro Mexicano de Escritores, Apartado Postal 1298, Mexico 1, D.F., Children's Books Mexico, a list of books for children in Spanish, (free).

Cohen, David, chm. American Association of School Librarians, 50 East Huron St., Chicago, IL 60611. Multi-ethnic Media: Selected Bibliographies, (free).

Contemporary Press, Box 1524, San Jose, CA 95109. Selected Free Materials, a list of materials and addresses ($1.50).

Dimitroff, Lillian. National Education Association, Division of Educational Technology, 1201 Sixteenth St., NW., Washington, DC 20036. An Annotated Bibliography of Audiovisual Materials Related to Understanding and Teaching Culturally Disadvantaged, (75¢).

Free Library of Philadelphia, 19th and Vine Sts., Philadelphia, PA 19103. To Be Black in America, a bibliographic essay arranged in broad categories; materials included suitable for use by junior and senior high school students, (free).

Glancy, Barbara Jean. American Federal of Teachers, AFL-CIO, 1012-14th St., NW., Washington, D.C. 20036. Children's Interracial Fiction, an annotated unselected bibliography identifying 328 books with black characters, ($1).

Information Center on Children's Cultures, United States Committee for UNICEF, 331 East 38th St., Ne York, NY 10016. Africa: An Annotated List of Printed Materials Suitable for Children, evaluation of all in-print English-language materials for children on the subject of Africa ($1).

_____. Latin America: An Annotated List of Materials for Children, evaluation of all in-print English-lanugage materials for children on the subject of Latin America, ($1).

Koblitz, Minnie. Center for Urban Education, 105 Madison Ave., New York, NY 10016. The Negro in Schoolroom Literature: Resource Materials for the Teacher of Kindergarten Through the 6th Grade, an annotated list of more than 250 books, background materials for teachers, source materials, author and publisher index, (25¢).

Michigan Department of Education, 735 East Michigan, Lansing, MI 49813. The Heritage of the Negro in America--a Bibliography: Books, Records Tapes Filmstrips, sources of information on contributions of the American Negro in various fields, (free).

National Education Association, 1201 Sixteenth St., NW., Washington, D.C. 20036. Index to Multiethnic Teaching Material and Teacher Resources, an annotated bibliography in four sections, (35¢).

New York Public Librry, Fifth Avenue and 42nd St., New York, NY 10018. A Touch of Soul, a selected, annotated listing of the most recent books for children, (free).

_____. Black Films: A Selected List, a film listing selected from the current film collection of the New York Library for a Black Films Workshop (free).

_____. Books, Films, Recordings By and About the American Negro, a selection of 233 titles, films tested with teenagers, recordings of various types of music styles plus recordings, (free).

Oakland Public Library, 1457 Fruitvale, Ave., Oakland, CA 94601. His House Below: Books from the Beach Struggle, an annotated list of media explaining the balck struggle, (free).

Pan American Union, 17th and Constitution Ave., NW., Washington, D.C. 20006. Proyecto Leer Bulletin, quarterly; lists elementary books and other reading audiovisual materials in Spanish for children and adults, (free).

Pennsylvania Department of Education, Bureau of Genral and Academic Education, Box 911, Harrisburg, PA 17126. American Diversity: A Bibliography of Resources on Racial and Ethnic Minorities for Pennsylvania Schools, an annotated, graded list identifying resources to implement curriculum studies relating to minority groups, (free).

Revelle, Keith. Latin American Library of the Oakland Public Library, 1457 Fruitvle Ave., Oakland, CA 94601. Chicana: A Selected Bibliography of Materials By and About Mexico and Mexican Americans, (free).

Rosenfeld, Harriet. Yeshiva University, Amsterdam Ave. and 186th St., New York, NW 10033. Books to Enhance the Self-Image of Negro Childred, an annotated list of 122 books organized in two parts on American life, Africa and the West Indies (free).

U.S. Committee for UNICEF, 331 East 38th t., New York, NW 10016. Photo Set: UNICEF's Children in School, twelve black and white photographs (12" x 14") with captions and illustrating UNICEF aid to education, ($1).

U.S. Department of the Interior, Bureau of Indian Affairs, Washington, D.C. 20240. Indian Bibliography, An annotated listing of part of the collection; contains books written by and about merican Indians, (free).

U.S. Office of Education, U.S. Government Printing Office, Washington, D.C. 20402. Books Related to Compensatory Education, a bibliography in three parts, concerning materials about Africa, minority groups, U.S. children with handicaps, (50¢).

Vogel, Virgil J. Integrated Education Associates, 343 South Dearborn St., Chicago, IL 60604. The Indian in American History, contributions of the American Indian to American

U.S. Department of the Interior, Bureau of Indian Affairs, Washington, D.C. 20240. Indian Bibliography, An annotated listing of part of the collection; contains books written by and about merican Indians, (free).

U.S. Office of Education, U.S. Government Printing Office, Washington, D.C. 20402. Books Related to Compensatory Education, a bibliography in three parts, concerning materials about Africa, minority groups, U.S. children with handicaps, (50¢).

Vogel, Virgil J. Integrated Education Associates, 343 South Dearborn St., Chicago, IL 60604. The Indian in American History, contributions of the American Indian to American civilization, (50¢).

Weinberg, Meyer. Integrated Education Associates, 343 Douth Dearborn St., Chicago, IL 60604. Afro-American History: Separate or Interracial? A commentary on Negro history, (50¢).

White, Doris, ERIC Clearinghouse on Early Childhood Education, 805 West Pennsylvania Ave., Urbana, IL 60801. Multi-Ethnic Books for Head Start Children: Black and Integrated Literature, an annotated list arranged by subject areas, (90¢).

LIBRARIES

"SELECTED OUTSTANDING ETHNIC PROGRAMS"

1. Atlanta Public Library (The)
   10 Pryor Street, S.W. Atlanta,
   Georgia 30303

   Contact: Janice Sikes
            Special Collection (Black) and/or
            Emma Estrada Spanish Project

2. Belen Public Library
   315 West Reinken Avenue
   Belen, New Mexico 87002

   "Hispanic & Indian Cultures"

   Contact: Dolores Padilla, Librarian

3. Britannia Public Library
   Britannia Community Services
   Centre 1661 Napier Street
   Vancouver, British Columbia

   "Multilingual Collections & Services"

   Contact: Pat Cook

4. Brooklyn Public Library
   El Centro Hispano de Informacion
   C/O Williamsburgh Regional Library
   240 Division Avenue
   Brooklyn, New York 11211

   Contact: Natalia G. Davis

5. Cambridge Public Library
   449 Broadway Cambridge,
   Massachusetts 02138
   Heritage of a City"

   Contact: Joseph G. Sakey

6. Chicago Public Library (The)
   425 North Michigan Avenue
   Chicago, Illinois 60611

   "America's Ethnic Heritage"
   Contact: Nazar H. Tiwana

7. Dallas Public Library
   1954 Commerce Street
   Dallas, Texas 75201

   "Hannuka"

   Contact: Frances Smardo

8. De Kalb Library System (The)
   3560 Kensington Road
   Decatur, Georgia 30032

   "Hispanic Collection"

9. Fresno County Free Library
   San Joaquin Valley Japanese-
   American Project
   2424 Mariposa Street
   Fresno, California 93721

   Contact: Mrs. Yoshino Hasega
             Project Director

10. Indian Center of San Jose, I
    3485 East Hills Drive
    San Jose, California 95127

    Contact: Ruth Blank, Librarian

11. Inland Library System
    Shared Chicano Resources Pro
    216 Brookside Avenue
    Redlands, California 92373

    Contact: George C. Elser

12. La Crosse Public Library
    800 Main Street
    La Cross, Wisconsin 54601

    "Winnebago Life & Culture"

    Contact: Carol Erickson

13. Langston Hughes Community
    Library & Cultural Center
    102-09 Northern Boulevard
    Corona, New York 11368

    Contact: Charlene Gadsden

14. Los Angeles County Public Library
    1550 West Beverly Boulevard
    Montebello, California 90640

    "Multilingual I & R"

    Contact: Marilyn Ayala

15. Miami-Dade Public Library
    Metropolitan Dade County
    One Biscayne Boulevard
    Miami, Florida 33132

    "Services to Non-English Speaking"

    Contact: Barbara E. Morris

16. Miami-Dade Public Library System
    Rama Hispanic Hispanic Branch
    2190 West Flagler Street
    Miami, Florida 33135

    Contact: Mrs. Ondina Arroyo

17. National City Public Library
    200 East 12th Street
    National City, California 92050

    "Hispanic Heritage Week"

    Contact: Ann L. Hartman

18. National Library of Canada
    Multilingual Biblioservice
    395 Wellington
    Ottawa, Canada K1A ON4

    Contact: Marie Zielinska, Chief

19. New England Library Board
    231 Capitol Avenue
    Hartford, Connecticut 06115

    "Ethnic Library Resources Directory"

    Contact: Sally B. Roberts

20. New York City Board of Education
    Division of Curriculum & Instruction
    Office of Library, Media & Telecommunication
    131 Livingston Street
    Brooklyn, New York 11201

21. Norwalk Public Library
    South Norwalk Branch
    10 Washington Street
    Norwarlk, Connecticut 06854

    "Hispanic Services"

    Contact: Janet Richer

22. Oakland Public Library
    Asian Community Library
    125 Fourteenth Street
    Oakland, California 94612

    Contact: Judy Yung

23. Oklahoma Image
    200 Northeast 18th Street
    Oklahoma City, Oklahoma 73105

    Contact: Ann Hodges Morgan

24. Public Library of Nashville &
     Davidson County (The)
     222 Eighth Avenue, North
     Nashville, Tennessee 37203

     "Services to Persons of Limited
     Engligh-Speaking Ability"

     Contact: Claudia Schauman

25. Queens Borough Public Library
     89-11 Merrick Boulevard
     Jamaica, New York 11432

     "New Americans Project"

     Contact: Adriana Tandler

26. Seattle Public Library
     1000 Fourth Avenue
     Seattle, Washington 98104

     "This City, Seattle"

     Contact: Jean Coberly

27. Toronto Public Library
     Metro Multilingual Operational Group
     40 Orchard View Boulevard
     Toronto, Ontario M4R 1B9

     Contact: Stephanie Hutcheson

28. Tucson Public Library (The)
             "Sonoran Heritage"
     City Hall Annex
     Post Office Box #27470
     Tucson, Arizona 85726

     "Museo de la Gente"

     Contact: Kathleen Dannreuther

29. University of Arizona (The)
    College of Education
    Graduate Library School
    1515 East First Street
    Tuscon, Arizona 85721

    "Graduate Library Institute for
    Spanish-Speaking Americans"

    Contact: Arnold D. Trejo

30. University of California,
    Los Angeles (The)
    Chicano Studies Center
    405 Hilgard Avenue
    Los Angeles, California 90024

31. University of California,
    Santa Barbara (The)
    Library
    Santa Barbara, California 93106

    "Coleccion Tloque Nahuaque"

    Contact: Roberto Trujillo

32. University of Guam
    College of Education
    Post Office Box #EK
    Agana, Guam 96910

    "Filipino Ethnic Materials"

    Contact: Mary Sue Caldwell

33. University of Pittsburgh Libraries
    Archives o Industrial Society
    Pittsburgh, Pennsylvania 15260

    "Survey of Ethnic Resources"

    Contact: Frank A. Zabrosky

34. Watertown Free Public Library (The)
    123 Main Street
    Watertown, Massachusetts 02172

    "Immigration/Acculturation of the
     Armenian Community"

    Contact: Stephen Bayle

Compiled by Natalia G. Davis

Director
Spanish Information Center
Williamsburg Branch
Brooklyn Public Library

Ethnic Materials Info.
Exchange Task Force
David Cohen, Coordinator
68-7, Bell Blvd.
Bayside, New York 11364

AFFIRMATIVE ACTION REGISTER
(Monthly)
Affirmative Action, Inc.
(For Effective Equal
Opportunity in Recruitment)
8356 Olive Blvd.
St. Louis, MO 63132
(314) 991-1335
Warren H. Green (ed)
Note: This publication
maintains listings of
available positions and
eligible applicants.Yearly
subscription--$15.00;
six-months--$8.00.

AGENDA
Communications Center of the
National Council of LaRaza
1721 Eye St., N.W. Suite 210
Washington, DC 20006
(202) 659-1251
Miguel Mendiville (ed)

AKWESASNE NOTES (Newsletter)
Program in American Studies of
the State University of New
York at Buffalo and D-Q
University (Davis,
California)
Mohawk Nation
Rooseveltown, NY 13683
(518) 358-9531
Note: Published five times
annually (March, May, July,
September, and December)

THE BILINGUAL JOURNAL
(Quarterly)
National Assessment and
Dissemination Center
ESEA Title VII
Lesley College
9 Mellen St.
Cambridge, MA 02138
Antonio Torres-Alcala (ed)

BILNGUAL REVIEW
Bilingual Review Press
York College
Department of Foreign
Languages
Jamaica, NY 11451
Gary Keller (ed)

BILL OF RIGHTS IN ACTION
(Quarterly)
(For High School and Adult
Education)
Constitutional Rights
Foundation
6310 San Vicente Blvd.
Los Angeles, CA 90048

AMERICAN HUNGARIAN EDUCATOR
(Newsletter)
American Hungarian Educators'
Association
P.O. Box 4103
Silver Spring, MD 20904

AMERICAN INDIAN CULTURE AND
RESEARCH JOURNAL
American Indian Culture Center
3220 Campbell Hall
University of California at
Los Angeles
Los Angeles, CA 90024

AMERICAN INDIAN JOURNAL
Institute for the Development
of Indian Law
927 15th St., N.W., Suite 200
Washington, DC 20005

AMERICAS (Monthly in Spanish,
English, and Portuguese)
Organization of American
States
Pan-American Union
Washington, DC 20006
Juan Vilaverde and Flora
Phelps (eds)

APPALACHIAN OUTLOOK
West Virginia University
Library, Main Office
Morgantown, WV 26506
Alice L. Dornemann (ed)

BLACK ENTERPRISE
Earl G. Graves Publishing Co.
295 Madison Ave.
New York, NY 10017
Phil W.Petrie (ed)

BLACK SCHOLAR
Black World Foundation
Box 908
Sausalito, CA 94965

THE BRIDGE: A JOURNAL OF
CROSS-CULTURAL AFFAIRS
(Quarterly)
The Center for Research and
Education
2010 E. 17th Ave.
Denver, CO 80206
(303) 388-6311
Collins Reynolds (ed)

143

THE BLACK COLLEGIAN
(The National Magazine of
Black College Students)
Black Collegiate Services,
Inc.
1240 S. Broad St.
New Orleans, LA 70125
(504) 821-5694
Kalamu ya Salaam (ed)
Note: Subscription
rate--$7.50

CITIZEN EDUCATION
Research For Better Schools,
Inc.
444 N. Third St.
Philadelphia, PA 19123

CIVIL RIGHTS DIGEST
Editor, Civil Rights Digest
U.S. Commission on Civil
Rights
Washington, DC 20425
Suzanne Crowell (ed)

CIVIL RIGHTS UPDATE
U.S. Commission On Civil
Rights
Washington, DC 20425
Roy Johnson (ed)

COMMENT (ON RESEARCH/ACTION
ABOUT WOMEN) (3 times per
year)
National Institute of
Education and Office of Women
in Higher Education
One Dupont Circle
Washington, DC 20036
Jo Hartley (ed)

COMMUNICATION QUARTERLY
Institute for Research on
Teaching
College of Education
Michigan State University
East Lansing, MI 48824
Linda D. F. Shalaway (ed)

CORE MAGAZINE (Congress of
Racial Equality)
CORE Publications
200 West 135 St.
New York, NY 10030
Denise Mitchell (ed)

EQUAL OPPORTUNITY REVIEW
Institute for Urban and
Minority Education
Teachers College
Columbia University
New York, NY 10027

CHILDHOOD EDUCATION
Association for Childhood
Education International
3615 Wisconsin Avenue, N.W.
Washington, DC 20016
Lucy Martin (ed)

CHRYSALIS (Quarterly)
(A Magazine of Women's
Culture)
Chrysalis
1727 N. Spring St.
Los Angeles, CA 90012
Kirsten Grimstad (ed)

DIALOGO (Quarterly)
Center For Latin American
Studies
University of Florida
Gainesville, FL 32611
Miriam Ocasio (ed)

EAST-WEST CENTER MAGAZINE
Office of Publication and
Public Affairs
East-West Center
1777 East-West Road
Honolulu, HI 96822
Mark E. Zeug (ed)

LA EDUCACION (Annually in
Spanish)
Organization of American
States
Education Department
Washington, DC 20006
Francisco Iglesias (ed)

EDUCATION AND URBAN SOCIETY
Sage Publications Inc.
275 South Beverly Drive
Beverly Hills, CA 90212

EPIC (Biannual Newsletter)
Northeastern State University
Tahlequah, OK 74464
Fount Holland, Wathene Young,
and Bill Thorne (eds)

EQUAL OPPORTUNITY FORUM
(Monthly)
Equal Opportunity Forum, Inc.
8240 Beverly Boulevard
Los Angeles, CA 90048
(213) 651-5617
Max Benavidez and Kathleen
Vozoff (eds)

FORUM (Newsletter)
National Clearinghouse for
Bilingual Education
1300 Wilson Boulevard, Suite
B2-11
Rosslyn, VA 22209

144

ETHNICITY (an
interdisciplinary journal of
the study of ethnic
relations)
Academic Press, Inc.
111 Fifth Avenue
New York, NY 10003
Andrew M. Greeley (ed)

THE EXCHANGE (A Quarterly
Journal of Native
American-Philanthropic News)
Native American-Philanthropic
News Service
Phelps-Stokes Fund
1029 Vermont Avenue, N.W.
Washington, DC 20005
Rose Robinson (ed)

FOCUS ON POVERTY RESEARCH
(Newsletter, three times per
year)
Institute for Research on
Poverty
3412 Social Science Bldg.
University of Wisconsin at
Madison
Madison, WI 53706
Katherine Mochon (ed)

FOMENTO LITERARIO (Spanish and
English Articles)
El Congreso Nacional de
Asuntos Colegiales
One Dupont Circle, NW Rm 410
Washington, DC 20036
Pepe Barron (ed)

I.C.E.E. HERITAGE (Newsletter)
Illinois Consultation on
Ethnicity in Education
Institute on Pluralism and
Group Identity
55 East Jackson Blvd., Suite
1880
Chicago, IL 60604
Nancy J. Siatka Rogalla (ed)

ICP NEWSLETTER (Bimonthly
Newsletter)
Institute for Cultural
Pluralism
5544 1/2 Hardy Ave.
San Diego, CA 92182
Ricardo Cornejo and Margarita
Calderon (eds)

IDRA NEWSLETTER (Monthly)
Intercultural Development and
Research Association
5835 Callaghan Rd., Suite 350
San Antonio, TX 58228
(512) 684-8180

HISPANA
American Association of
Teachers of Spanish and
Portuguese
Department of Modern Languages
Holy Cross College
Worcester, MA 01610
Donald W.Bleznick (ed)

HISPANIC AMERICAN HISTORICAL
REVIEW
Duke University Press
Box 6697
College Station
Durham, NC 27708
Michael C. Meyer (ed)

HUMAN RESOURCES ABSTRACTS
Sage Publications Inc.
275 South Beverly Drive
Beverly Hills, CA 90212

HUMANIDADES (Quarterly
Newsletter)
Puerto Rico Endowment For The
Humanities
P.O. Box S-4307
San Juan, PR 00904
Francisco J. Carreras
(President)

INTEGRATED EDUCATION
(Bimonthly)
School of Education
Northwestern University
2003 Sheridan Rd.
Evanston, IL 60201
(312) 492-9465
Meyer Weinberg (ed)

INTERNATIONAL AND
INTERCULTURAL COMMUNICATION
ANNUAL
Speech Communication
Association
Statler Hilton Hotel
New York, NY 10001

INTERNATIONAL JOURNAL OF
INTERCULTURAL RELATIONS
Pergamon Press, Inc.
Fairview Park
Elmsford, NY 10523
Dan Landis (ed)

145

IN THE RUNNING (Newsletter)
SPRINT (A National
Clearinghouse of Information
on Sex Equity in Sports)
805 15th St., NW, Suite 822
Washington, DC 20005
(202) 638-1961
Carol Parr (Executive
Director)

INEQUALITY IN EDUCATION
Center for Law and Education,
Inc.
Gutman Library
6 Appian Way
Cambridge, MA 02138
Sharon Schumack (ed)

IRCD BULLETIN
Institute for Urban and
Minority Education
Teachers College
Columbia University
Box 40, 525 West 120th St.
New York, NY 10027
Edmund W. Gordon (ed)

JEWISH EDUCATION
National Council for Jewish
Education
114 Fifth Ave.
New York, NY 10011
Alvin Schiff (ed)

JOURNAL OF AFRO-AMERICAN
ISSUES
Educational and Community
Counselors Associates
1629 K St., NW, Suite 520
Washington, DC 20006

JOURNAL OF AMERICAN INDIAN
EDUCATION
Arizona State University
College of Education
Bureau of Educational Research
and Services
Tempe, AZ 85281
George A. Gill (ed)

JOURNAL OF BLACK STUDIES
Sage Publications, Inc.
275 S. Beverly Dr.
Beverly Hills, CA 90212
Molefi Kete (ed)

JOURNAL OF ETHNIC STUDIES
Western Washington University
College of Ethnic Studies
Bellingham, WA 98225

INTERNATIONAL MIGRATION REVIEW
(Quarterly)
Center for Migration Studies
209 Flagg Place
Staten Island, NY 10304

INTERRACIAL BOOKS FOR CHILDREN
BULLETIN
Council on Interracial Books
for Children
1841 Broadway
New York, NY 10023
Bradford Chambers (ed)

INTERRACIAL DIGEST
Council on Interracial Books
for Children
1841 Broadway
New York, NY 10023
Ruth Charnes (ed)

JOURNAL OF INTERGROUP
RELATIONS
National Association of Human
Rights Workers
526 West 39th St.
Kansas City, MO 64111
Griffin Crump (ed)

THE JOURNAL OF NEGRO EDUCATION
Howard University Press
Howard University
Washington, DC 20059
Charles A. Martin (ed)

JOURNAL OF NEGRO HISTORY
Association for the Study of
Afro-American Life and
History
1407 14th St., NW
Washington, DC 20005
Alton Hornsby (ed)

JOURNAL OF NON-WHITE CONCERNS
IN PERSONNEL AND GUIDANCE
American Personnel and
Guidance Association
1607 New Hampshire Ave., NW
Washington, DC 20009
Ed Maggie (ed)

JOURNAL OF TEACHER EDUCATION
American Association of
Colleges for Teacher
Education
One Dupont Circle, Suite 610
Washington, DC 20036
(202) 293-2450
Martin Haberman (ed)

LATCA (A Magazine of Latino
  Awareness in the Midwest)
Indiana University
LaCasa/Latino Center
Bloomington, IN 47401
(812) 337-0174
Jack Ramos Needham (ed)

LAW AND CONTEMPORARY PROBLEMS
Duke University School of Law
Duke University Press
Durham, NC 27706
Melvin G. Shimm

LEGAL MEMORANDUM
National Association of
  Secondary School Principals
1904 Association Dr.
Reston, VA 22091
Thomas F. Koerner (ed)

THE LINGUISTIC REPORTER
  (Newsletter)
Center for Applied Linguistics
1611 N. Kent St.
Arlington, VA 22209
(703) 528-4312
JoAnn Crandall (ed)

METAS
Aspira of America
205 Lexington Ave.
New York, NY 10016
Kal Wagenheim (ed)

MEXICAN NEWSLETTER (Monthly)
Mexican Newletter
Palma No. 40-5o. piso
Mexico 1, D.F., Mexico

MIGRATION TODAY (Bimonthly
  Newsletter)
Center for Migration Studies
209 Flagg Place
Staten Island
New York, NY 10304

NETWORK (Quarterly)
National Urban Coalition
1201 Connecticut Ave., NW
Washington, DC 20036
(202) 331-2413
Stephanie Drea (ed)

NEW DIRECTIONS (Quarterly)
Howard University
Department of University
  Relations and Publications
Washington, DC 20059

MINORITY NEWS DIGEST
Minority News Digest, Inc.
No. 2 East 37th St.
New York, NY 10016
(212) 683-6363
Clemencio A. McKoy (ed)

MONITOR
Institute for the Study of
  Educational Policy
2935 Upton St., NW
Washington, DC 20008
Earnestine Stripling (ed)

MOSAIC
Institute of Intercultural
  Relations and Ethnic Studies
Rutgers University, GSE
10 Seminary Place
New Brunswick, NJ 08903
Eliane C. Condon and Madelyn
  Milchman (ed)

MULTICULTURALISM (Quarterly)
University of Toronto Faculty
  of Education and the
  Multicultural Development
  Branch of the Ministry of
  Culture and Recreation of
  Ontario
371 Bloor St., West
Toronto, Ontario, Canada M4W
  2K8
Keith A. McLeod (ed)

NEA REPORTER
National Education Association
1201 16th St., NW
Washington, DC 20036
Marshall O. Donley, Jr.(ed)

NEGRO EDUCATIONAL REVIEW
Box 2895
West Bay Annex
Jacksonville, FL 32216
R. Grann Lloyd (ed)

REPORT CARD ON INTEGRATION
  (Monthly Newsletter)
The Center for the Advancement
  of Integrated Education
7 East 96th St.
New York, NY 10028

REPORT ON EDUCATION RESEARCH
Capitol Publications, Inc.
Suite G-12, 2430 Pennsylvania
  Ave., NW
Washington, DC 20037
(202) 452-1600

NEWSLETTER
Asian American Bilingual
 Center
2168 Shattuck Ave., 3/F
Berkeley, CA 94704
Note: ESEA Publication, Title
 VII National Network of
 Centers for Bilingual
 Education

NEWSNOTES
The Feminist Press
Box 334
Old Westbury, NY 11568
Phyllis Arlow (ed)
Note: Irregular Publication

PEER PERSPECTIVE
Project on Equal Education
 Rights
1029 Vermont Ave., NW, Suite
 800
Washington, DC 20005
(202) 332-7337

SEX ROLES: A JOURNAL OF
 RESEARCH
Plenum Press
227 W. 17th St.
New York, NY 10011
Phyllis A. Katz (ed)

SIETAR COMMUNIQUE (Quarterly
 Newsletter)
Society for Intercultural
 Education, Training, and
 Research
Georgetown University
Washington, DC 20057
Diane L. Zeller (ed)

SOCIAL EDUCATION
National Council for the
 Social Studies
1515 Wilson Blvd.
Arlington, VA 22209
Daniel Roselle (ed)

SOCIAL POLICY
Social Policy Corp.
Suite 500, 184 Fifth Ave.
New York, NY 10010
Frank Riessman (ed)

SPECTRUM
Immigration History Research
 Center
University of Minnesota .
826 Berry St.
St. Paul, MN 55114

REPORT ON THE EDUCATION OF THE
 DISADVANTAGED
Capitol Publications, Inc.
Education News Services
 Division
Suite G-12, 2430 Pennsylvania
 Ave., NW
Washington, DC 20037
Helen Hoart (ed)

RESEARCH REVIEW OF EQUAL
 EDUCATION (Quarterly)
Center for Equal Education
School of Education
University of Massachusetts
Amherst, MA 01003
(413) 545-0327
Meyer Weinberg (ed)

SCHOOLS and CIVIL RIGHTS NEWS
 (Biweekly Newsletter)
Capitol Publications, Inc.
Suite G-12, 2430 Pennsylvania
 Ave., NW
Washington, DC 20037

T.E.S.O.L. QUARTERLY
Teachers of English to
 Speakers of Other Languages
c/o James E. Alatis
School of Languages and
 Linguistics
Georgetown University
Washington, DC 20057

UN NUEVO DIA
The Chicano Education Project
5410 W. Mississippi
Lakewood, CO 80226
(303) 922-6371
Nancy De La Rosa and Lydia
 Urioste (eds)

URBAN AFFAIRS QUARTERLY
Sage Publications, Inc.
275 S. Beverly, Dr.
Beverly Hills, CA 90212
Louis Masotti (ed)

URBAN EDUCATION
Sage Publications, Inc.
275 S. Beverly Dr.
Beverly Hills, cA 90212
Warren Button (ed)

URBAN LIFE (A JOURNAL OF
 ETHNOGRAPHIC RESEARCH)
Sage Publications, Inc.
275 S. Beverly Dr.
Beverly Hills, CA 90212

TEACHING EXCEPTIONAL CHILDREN
Council for Exceptional
 Children
1920 Association Dr.
Reston, VA 22091
June B. Jordan (ed)

URBAN REVIEW
APS Publications
150 Fifth Ave.
New York, NY 10011
David E. Kapel and William
 T. Pink (eds)

WOMEN TODAY
Today Publications and News
 Service, Inc.
621 National Press Bldg.
Washington, DC 20045
Myra E. Barrer (ed)

WOMEN'S WORK
Women's Work, Inc.
1302 18th St., NW, Suite 203
Washington, DC 20036

ORGANIZATION RESOURCES

THE AFRICAN-AMERICAN INSTITUTE
833 United Nations Plaza
New York, NY 10017
(212) 949-5666
Contact: Donald Easum,
 President

ALASKAN NATIVE LANGUAGE
MATERIAL DEVELOPMENT CENTER
University of Alaska
2223 Spenard Rd.
Anchorage, AK 99503
(907) 276-0547
Contact: Tupou Pulu

AMANECER (Multicultural Action
 Network for Early Childhood
 Educational Resources)
 I.D.R.A.
5835 Callaghan Rd., Suite 350
San Antonio, TX 78228 Contact:
 Jose A. Cardenas, Executive
 Director

AMERICAN ASSOCIATION OF
 UNIVERSITY WOMEN
2401 Virginia Ave., NW,
Washington, DC 20037

THE AMERICAN HUNGARIAN
 EDUCATOR'S ASSOCIATION
707 Snider Lane
Silver Spring, MD 20904
(301) 426-6323
Contact: Eniko M. Base

ASIAN BILINGUAL CURRICULUM
 DEVELOPMENT CENTER (CHINESE)
Seton Hall University
440 South Orange Ave.
South Orange, NJ 07070
(201) 762-9000 or 762-4973

AMERICAN INDIAN STUDIES CENTER
(Native North American
 Languages)
University of California
Campbell Hall, Rm. 3220
405 Hilgard Ave.
Los Angeles, CA 90024
(213) 825-7315
Contact: Karin Abbey

ANTI-DEFAMATION LEAGUE OF
 B'NAI B'RITH
315 Lexington Ave.
New York, NY 10016

ARIZONA TITLE VII BILINGUAL
 MATERIALS DEVELOPMENT CENTER
College of Education
Box 601
University of Arizona
Tucson, AZ 85721
(602) 626-1618

ARMENIAN LANGUAGE LAB AND
 RESOURCE CENTER
Diocese of the Armenian Church
 of America
630 Second Ave.
New York, NY 10016
(212) 696-0710
Contact: Sylva Der Stepanian

ASIAN AMERICAN BILINGUAL
 CENTER
2168 Shattuck Avenue
Berkeley, CA 94704

BILINGUAL BICULTURAL EDUCATION
 (Title VII Tagalog Center)
Oakland Unified School
 District
831 East 14th
Oakland, CA 94606

149

CENTER FOR APPLIED
LINGUISTICS
1611 North Kent St.
Arlington, VA 22209
(703) 528-4312
Contact: Rudolph C. Troike,
Director

THE CENTER FOR THE ADVANCEMENT
OF INTEGRATED EDUCATION
7 East 96th St.
New York, NY 10028

CENTER FOR MIGRATION STUDIES
209 Flagg Place
Staten Island, NY 10304
Publishers of INTERNATIONAL
MIGRATION REVIEW (Quarterly)
and MIGRATION TODAY
(Bimonthly)

CENTER FOR TEACHING
INTERNATIONAL RELATIONS
Graduate School of
International Studies
University of Denver
Denver, CO 80210

CENTER FOR THE STUDY OF
EVALUATION
145 Moore Hall
University of California
Los Angeles, CA 90024

COUNCIL ON INTERRACIAL BOOKS
FOR CHILDREN
1841 Broadway
New York, NY 10023

THE DANISH BROTHERHOOD IN
AMERICA
Fraternal Affairs Department
3717 Harney St.
Omaha, NE 68131
(402) 341-5049

DATA USE AND ACCESS
LABORATORIES, INC.
National Ethnic Statistical
Data Guidance Service
1601 North Kent St.
Arlington, VA 22209
(703) 525-1480

CHICANO STUDIES CENTER
University of California at
Los Angeles
Los Angeles, CA 90024
Publishers of AZTLAN and
INTERNATIONAL JOURNAL OF
CHICANO STUDIES MONOGRAPHS

THE COALITION RESOURCE CENTER
(Native North American
Languages)
Coalition of Indian Controlled
School Boards
511 16th St.
Denver, CO 80202
(303) 573-5715

COMMISSION FOR RACIAL EQUALITY
Elliot House
10-12 Allington Street
London SW1E 5EH

COMMUNITY RELATIONS COMMISSION
15-16 Bedford Street
London WC2E 9HX

COUNCIL FOR EXCEPTIONAL
CHILDREN
1920 Association Drive
Reston, VA 22091

THE DISSEMINATION CENTER FOR
THE PRODUCTS OF THE WOMEN'S
EDCATIONAL EQUITY ACT PROGRAM
(U.S. Department of HEW,
Office of Education)
c/o Education Development
Center
55 Chapel St.
Newton, MA 02160
(617) 969-7100 Or toll free
(800) 225-3088

ERIC (EDUCATIONAL RESOURCES
INFORMATION CENTER)
U.S. Department of Health,
Education & Welfare,
National Institute of
Education
Washington, DC 20208

ERIC CLEARINGHOUSE ON ADULT,
CAREER, & VOCATIONAL
EDUCATION
Ohio State University
National Center for Research
in Vocational Education
1960 Kenny Rd.
Columbus, OH 43210
(614) 486-3655

ERIC CLEARINGHOUSE ON
COUNSELING & PERSONNEL
SERVICES
University of Michigan
School of Education Bldg.,
Rm. 2108
Ann Arbor, MI 48109
(313) 764-9492

ERIC CLEARINGHOUSE ON
EDUCATIONAL MANAGEMENT
University of Oregon
Eugene, OR 97403
(503) 686-5043

ERIC CLEARINGHOUSE ON
ELEMENTARY & EARLY CHILDHOOD
EDUCATION
University of Illinois
College of Education
Urbana, IL 61801
(217) 333-1386

ERIC CLEARINGHOUSE ON
HANDICAPPED & GIFTED CHILDREN
Council for Exceptional
Children
1920 Association Dr.
Reston, VA 22091
(703) 620-3660

ERIC CLEARINGHOUSE ON HIGHER
EDUCATION
George Washington University
One Dupont Circle, Suite 630
Washington, DC 20036
(202) 296-2597

ERIC CLEARINGHOUSE FOR SOCIAL
STUDIES/SOCIAL SCIENCE
EDUCATION
855 Broadway
Boulder, CO 80302
(303) 492-8434

ERIC CLEARINGHOUSE ON TEACHER
EDUCATION
American Association of
Colleges for Teacher
Education
One Dupont Circle, Suite 616
Washington, DC 20036
(202) 293-2450

ERIC CLEARINGHOUSE ON
INFORMATION RESOURCES
Syracuse University
School of Education
130 Huntington Hall
Syracuse, NY 13210
(315) 423-3640

ERIC CLEARINGHOUSE FOR JUNIOR
COLLEGES
University of California
Powell Library, Rm. 96
405 Hilgard Ave.
Los Angeles, CA 90024
(213) 825-3931

ERIC CLEARINGHOUSE ON
LANGUAGES & LINGUISTICS
Center for Applied Linguistics
1611 North Kent St.
Arlington, VA 22209
(703) 528-4312

ERIC CLEARINGHOUSE ON READING
& COMMUNICATION SKILLS
National Council of Teachers
of English
1111 Kenyon Rd.
Urbana, IL 61801
(217) 328-3870

ERIC CLEARINGHOUSE ON RURAL
EDUCATION & SMALL SCHOOLS
New Mexico State University
Box 3 AP
Las Cruces, NM 88003
(505) 646-2623

ERIC CLEARINGHOUSE FOR
SCIENCE, MATHEMATICS, &
ENVIRONMENTAL EDUCATION
Ohio State University
1200 Chambers Rd., Third Floor
Columbus, OH 43212
(614) 422-6717

FAR WEST LABORATORY FOR
EDUCATIONAL RESEARCH AND
DEVELOPMENT
1855 Folsom St.
San Francisco, CA 94103
(415) 565-3000
Contact: John Hemphill,
Director

FEDERAL COMMUNICATIONS
COMMISSION
1919 M St., NW
Washington, DC 20554
(202) 632-7260--general info.
(202) 632-0002--for recorded
listing of releases and texts

ERIC CLEARINGHOUSE ON TESTS,
MEASUREMENT, & EVALUATION
Educational Testing Service
Rosedale Rd.
Princeton, NJ 08541
(609) 921-9000, ext. 2176

ERIC CLEARINGHOUSE ON URBAN
EDUCATION
Teachers College, Columbia
University
Box 40
525 W. 120th St.
New York, NY 10027
(212) 678-3437

ETHNIC HERITAGE STUDIES
CLEARINGHOUSE
Social Science Education
Consortium
855 Broadway
Boulder, CO 80302
(303) 492-8154

HEARTLAND EDUCATION AGENCY
(Title VII, Laotian)
1932 SW Third St.
Ankeny, IA 50021
(515) 964-2550
Contact: Richard Murphy

IMMIGRATION HISTORY RESEARCH
CENTER
University of Minnesota
826 Berry St.
St. Paul, MN 55114
(612) 373-5581
Contact: Rudolph J. Vecoli,
Director

IMPACT PUBLISHERS
PO 1094
San Luis Obispo, CA 93406

THE INDIAN EDUCATION PROGRAM
(Native North American
Languages)
Center for Applied Linguistics
1611 North Kent St.
Arlington, VA 22209
(703) 528-4312
Contact: William Leap

INDIAN EDUCATION RESOURCE
CENTER (Native North American
Languages)
Indian Education Resource
Center
Bureau of Indians Affairs
P.O. Box 1788
Albuquerque, NM 87103

THE FEMINIST PRESS
PO Box 334
Old Westbury, NY 11568

FORT HAMILTON HIGH SCHOOL
8301 Shore Road
Brooklyn, NY 11209
(212) 748-1018
Contact: Gertrude Burns

THE FOUNDATION CENTER
1001 Connecticut Ave., NW
Washington, DC 20036
(202) 331-1400

or

888 7th Ave.
New York, NY 10019
(212) 975-1120

FOUNDATION FOR CHANGE, INC.
1841 Broadway
New York, NY 10019

INSTITUTE FOR THE STUDY OF
EDUCATIONAL POLICY
Howard University, Dumbarton
Campus
2935 Upton St., NW
Washington, DC 20008
(202) 686-6686
Contact: Paul Brock

INSTITUTE ON PLURALISM AND
GROUP IDENTITY
The American Jewish Committee
165 East 56th St.
New York, NY 10022

INTERCULTURAL DEVELOPMENT
RESEARCH ASSOCIATES
5835 Callaghan Road, Suite 350
San Antonio, TX 78228

INTERCULTURAL NETWORK, INC.
906 North Spring Ave.
LaGrange Park, IL 60525
(312) 579-0646
Contact: Margaret D. Pusch,
Executive Director

INTERNATIONAL CENTER FOR
RESEARCH ON BILINGUALISM
L'University Laval
P.O. Box 2447
Quebec, Canada

INTERNATIONAL READING
ASSOCIATION
800 Barksdale Road
Newark, DE 19711

INSTITUTE FOR AMERICAN INDIAN
ARTS
Research and Cultural Studies
Development Section
Cerillos Road
Santa Fe, NM 87501
(505) 988-6486
Contact: Dave Warren

JAPANESE AMERICAN CURRICULUM
PROJECT, INC. (Title VII)
414 East Third Ave.
P.O. Box 367
San Mateo, CA 94401
(415) 343-9408

THE LEARNING TREE
9998 Ferguson Road
Dallas, TX 75228

LIBRARIES UNLIMITED
Box 263
Littleton, CO 80120

LIBRARY OF CONGRESS
1st & Independence Ave., SE
Washington, DC 20540
(202) 287-5000

MAGEN DAVID YESHIVA (Hebrew)
50 Ave. "P"
Brooklyn, NY 11204
(212) 236-5905
Contact: Bonnie Hendel

MICHIGAN ETHNIC HERITAGE
STUDIES CENTER
Wayne State University
197 Manoogian Hall
Detroit, MI 48202

MIDWEST OFFICE FOR MATERIALS
DEVELOPMENT (Vietnamese)
805 West Pennsylvania Ave.,
3rd Floor
University of Illinois
Urbana, IL 61801
(217) 333-2615

NATIONAL ASSOCIATION OF
INTERDISCIPLINARY ETHNIC
STUDIES
101 Main Hall
University of Wisconsin-La
Crosse
La Crosse, WI 54601

NATIONAL ASSOCIATION OF
MEXICAN AMERICAN EDUCATORS
2717 Winthrop Ave.
Arcadia, CA 91006
(213) 245-1000

JAPAN INFORMATION SERVICE
280 Park Ave.
New York, NY 10017
Contact: Consulate General of
Japan

MOUNTAIN VIEW-LOS ALTOS
UNIFIED HIGH SCHOOL DISTRICT
(Title VII, Ilokano)
1299 Bryant St.
Mountain View, CA 94040
(415) 967-5543
Contact: Robert McLennan

MULTICULTURAL RESOURCES
Box 2945
Stanford, CA 94305

NATIONAL ASSESSMENT AND
DISSEMINATION CENTER (TITLE
VII)
385 High Street
Fall River, MA 02720

NATIONAL ASSESSMENT OF
EDUCATION PROGRESS
Education Commission of the
States
1860 Lincoln St., Suite 700
Denver, CO 80295

NATIONAL ASSOCIATION FOR
BILINGUAL EDUCATION (NABE)
IU-13 BESL Center
100 Franklin St.
New Holland, PA 17557
(717) 354-7737
Contact: Ramon L. Santiago

NATIONAL ASSOCIATION FOR EQUAL
OPPORTUNITY IN HIGHER
EDUCATION
2001 S St., NW
Washington, DC 20009
(202) 232-9500

NATIONAL COUNCIL OF TEACHERS
OF ENGLISH
1111 Kenyon Road
Urbana, IL 61801

NATIONAL EDUCATION ASSOCIATION
1201 16th Street, NW
Washington, DC 20036
(202) 833-4000

NATIONAL EDUCATION LAB
PUBLICATIONS
813 Airport Blvd.
Austin, TX 78708

THE NATIONAL CENTER FOR
RESEARCH IN VOCATIONAL
EDUCATION
The Ohio State University
1960 Kenny Road
Columbus, OH 43210

NATIONAL CENTER FOR URBAN
ETHNIC AFFAIRS
1521 16th Street, NW
Washington, DC

NATIONAL CLEARINGHOUSE FOR
BILINGUAL EDUCATION
1500 Wilson Boulevard, Suite
802
Rosslyn, VA 22209
(703) 522-0710 or Hot Line
(800) 336-4560

NATIONAL CONFERENCE OF
CHRISTIANS AND JEWS
43 W. 57th Street
New York, NY

NATIONAL COUNCIL FOR
ACCREDITATION OF TEACHER
CERTIFICATION
1750 Pennylvania Ave., NW,
Suite 411
Washington, DC 20006

NATIONAL ORGANIZATION OF WOMEN
(NOW)
425 13th St.
Washington, DC
(202) 347-2279

NATIONAL SUPPORT SYSTEMS
PROJECT
253 Burton Hall
University of Minnesota
Minneapolis, MN 55455
(612) 373-4854
Contact: Maynard C. Reynolds

NATIONAL TASK FORCE ON
DESEGREGATION STRATEGIES
Education Commission of the
States
1860 Lincoln St., Suite 300
Denver, CO 80295
(303) 861-4917
Contact: Ben Williams,
Director

NATIONAL TITLE VII
DISSEMINATION AND ASSESSMENT
CENTER
California State University,
Los Angeles
5151 State University Dr.
Los Angeles, CA 90032

THE NATIONAL FOUNDATION FOR
THE IMPROVEMENT OF EDUCATION
1156 15th Street, NW, Suite
918
Washington, DC 20005

NATIONAL INDIAN EDUCATION
ASSOCIATION
3036 University Ave., SE
Minneapolis, MN 55414

NATIONAL INDOCHINESE
CLEARINGHOUSE AND TECHNICAL
ASSISTANCE CENTER (NIC/TAC)
Center for Applied Linguistics
1611 North Kent St.
Arlington, VA 22209
(703) 528-4312 or Hot Line
(800) 336-3040
Contact: Allene G. Grognet

NATIONAL INSTITUTE OF
EDUCATION
U. S. Department of HEW
Washington, DC 20208

THE NATIONAL HUMANITIES
FACULTY
1266 Main Street
Concord, MA 01742

NEW ENGLAND
MULTILINGUAL-MULTICULTURAL
TEACHING RESOURCE CENTER,
(Title VII)
Bilingual Program
86 Fourth St.
Povidence, RI 02906
(401) 272-4900, exts. 293, 297

OFFICE FOR ADVANCEMENT OF
PUBLIC NEGRO COLLEGES
National Association of State
Universities & Land-Grant
Colleges
805 Peachtree St., NE
Atlanta, GA 30308
(404) 874-8073

OFFICE OF COPYRIGHT
Copyright Office
Library of Congress
Washington, DC 20559
(703) 557-8700

NATIVE AMERICAN MATERIALS
DEVELOPMENT CENTER (Title
VII)
407 Rio Grande Boulevard, NW
Albuquerque, NM 87104
(505) 242-5222

PEER (PROJECT ON EQUAL
EDUCATION RIGHTS)
NOW Legal Defense & Education
Fund
1029 Vermont Ave., NW, Suite
800
Washington, DC 20005
(202) 332-7337
Contact: Holly Knox

PINELLAS COUNTY SCHOOLS (Title
VII)
Curriculum and Instruction
Center
205 4th St., SW
Largo, FL 33540
(813) 585-9951
Contact: Maria Sanchez

PRAEGER SPECIAL STUDIES
383 Madison Ave.
New York, NY 10017

PROJECT BEST
Bilingual Education Applied
Research Unit
Hunter College
560 Lexington Ave.
New York, NY 10022
Contact: Marietta Saravia
Shore, Coordinator

R & E RESEARCH ASSOCIATES,
INC.
936 Industrial Ave.
Palo Alto, CA 94303

RESOURCE CENTER FOR ITALIAN
(Title VII)
Public School #97
Ave. "S" & Stillwell Ave.
Brooklyn, NY 11223
(212) 372-7393
Contact: Mrs. Paul Alleva

SOUTHERN REGIONAL EDUCATION
BOARD
130 Sixth Street, NW
Atlanta, GA 30313

SPEECH COMMUNICATION
ASSOCIATION
5205 Leesburg Pike, Suite 1000
Falls Church, VA 22041
(703) 879-1888

SPRINT
Women's Equity Action League
Educational & Legal Defense
Fund
805 Fifteenth St., NW, Suite
822
Washington, DC 20005
(202) 638-1961

RESOURCE CENTER FOR RUSSIAN
(Title VII)
Public School #225
1075 Oceanview Ave.
Brooklyn, NY 11235
(212) 743-9793 or 266-1733
Contact: Emil Bednar or Gina
Sullivan

RESOURCE AND REFERRAL SERVICE
(Part of the Research &
Development Exchange,
National Institute of
Education)
The Ohio State University
1960 Kenny Road
Columbus, OH 43210
(614) 486-3655
Contact: John C. Peterson

ROMANIAN LIBRARY
200 East 38th St.
New York, NY 10016
Contact: Ion Monafu,
Executive Secretary

THE SCHOMBURG CENTER FOR
RESEARCH IN BLACK CULTURE
103 West 135th St.
New York, NY 10030
(212) 862-4000
Contact: Otillia Pearson

SOCIAL SCIENCE EDUCATION
CONSORTIUM
855 Broadway
Boulder, CO 80203

SOUTH SHORE HIGH SCHOOL (Title
VII, Russian)
Bilingual Education
6565 Flatlands Ave.
Brooklyn, NY 11236
(212) 531-4454
Contact: Anna Elman

TELECOMMUNICATIONS CONSUMER
COALITION
105 Madison Ave., Suite 921
New York, NY 10016
(212) 683-5656
Contact: Ralph M. Jennings,
Executive Director

TITLE VII ASSESSMENT AND
DISSEMINATION CENTER
(Includes Pacific Area
Languages)
California State University -
Los Angeles
5151 State University Drive
Los Angeles, CA 90032
(213) 224-3676
Contact: Charles Leyba

Appendix

Although it is impossible to review all the court rulings
and federal laws pertaining to teacher and student rights, it is
important that you be aware of both your legal rights and responsibilities as a teacher as well as those of your students. The
following are a summary of the Case Analysis Exercises that you
found in Section 4.

Case Analysis # 1: Unless there is an applicable state law requiring provision of resources to supplement biased textbooks, this
is probably an issue that is "beyond the law."

Case Analysis #2: First Amendment, Title IX   This issue has
been raised in several states. The overriding factor in each case
is the student's First Amendment rights to practice their religion
without or with little interference from the state. For example,
in the U.S. District Court for Souther Illinois, Moody v. Cronin,
it was argued that Title IX allows students to be excused from
certain coed classes because of religious objections. The Illinois
State Department of Education argued that the gym attire is not
immodest by modern standards and that the state's interest in
having students attend classes outweighs the student's First
Amendment claims. In other cases, separate P.E. classes were provided for the student in order to protect their religous freedom and
insure they met the state graduation requirements which could not
be waived.

Case Analysis #3: Title IX, Title VII of OCR and E.O. 11246
The linking of job qualifications that would result in a disparate
impact on the employment opportunties of members of one sex is pro-
hibited by Title IX and Title VII. However, this type of situation
has given great concern and the courts have been very unclear as
to the final ruling.

Case Analysis #4: Title VI of the Civil Rights Act
The assignment of students to courses or the imposition of testing
or evaluation requirements upon students on the basis of their
race is discriminatory and in violation of the above laws.

Case Analysis #5: First Amendment, Title VII
Ms. Herriot argued she had constitutional rights to pursue religion.
The school district based her dismissal on the argument that her

students cannot be expected to give up their right to certain parts of their education to insure her religious freedom. The U.S. Supreme Court left intact a federal appeals court ruling which upheld her dismissal.

In another case, the Supreme Court overturned the firing of a teacher because he wanted seven or eight days off during the school year to attend religious observances. The Court said it would not present a hardship to the District to get a subsititute and insure his right to religious freedom.

Case Analysis #6:   P.L. 94-142; Title VI of 1964 Civil Rights Act; Title VI of Elementary and Secondary Act (Bilingual Ed); Lau v. Nichols, U.S. Supreme Court 1974.

According to P.L. 94-142, a child must be evaluated in order to be placed in a special education setting. It is also the school's responsibility to place a student in the most appropriate setting. In this case, the student should be placed in a regular classroom and then tested to determine what her English speaking ability is. She should receive adequate instruction in English, appropriate to her level, as well as reading, spelling and other basic skills.

Case Analysis #7: Section 86.34 of Title IX - Access to Course Offerings - states no educational program or activity may be carried out separately on the basis of sex.

Case Analysis #8:   Title IX and the Fourteenth Amendment to the U.S. Constitution.

Title IX prohibits discrimination on the basis of sex against students of a school receiving federal financial assistance. In the examples cited, the school could be discriminating in the application of rules of appearance. Can girls wear earrings? Can girls wear shoulder-length hair? Sandra is covered by the Fourteenth Amendment: "No state shall make or enforce any which shall abridge the privileges or immunities of citizens of the United States; nor shall any state deprive any person of life, liberty, or property without due process of law; nor deny any person within its jurisdiction the equal protection of the laws."

Case Analysis #9:   Title VII, Equal Pay Act, Pregnancy Discrimination Act

It is unlawful for covered institutions to :
* deny employees the right to use their sick leave for pregnancy related leave
*place limits on maternity leave
*require employees to ask for leave lone in advance(unless same is asked of other employees with other temporary disabilities)
*require doctor's permission to continue teaching unless required of all
* offer health insurance requiring a deductible for pregnancy

* have a separate reimbursement schedule for pregnancy and childbirth which is not comparable to other temporary disabilities.

Ms. Johnson has worked seven years for the District and has probably accumulated substantial sick leave. The school district is
obligated to let her use this for maternity leave and pay her accordingly.

Case Analysis #10: P.L. 94-142 and Rehabilitation Act of 1973
Physical education should be offered for handicapped children in
the most integrated setting possible. Also, separation of these
students from other students during lunch or recreation may deny
the students the benefits of association with other students. An
adaptive physical education class might be appropriate in this
situation.

Case Analysis #11: Title VI of Civil Rights Act of 1964, Lau v.
Nichols
A school district can be in jeopardy of losing its federal funding
if it does not provide adequate language instruction (sufficient
to insure equal educational opportunity) to limited English- speaking students after adequate testing to find out their current skill
level in English.

Case Analysis #12: First Amendment
The school district is obligated to change its current practice.
Public tax dollars cannot pay for a building used by a church. This
can be accomplished in several different ways:
*Bible study can be changed to nonschool hours
*Class c an be conducted in a nonschool building
*Students can be excused from class for two hours a week (as long
as this does not interfere with their meeting required academic
subjects.
*** Of course, this particular situation is being tested in the
courts today with the movement of "voluntary prayer in the schools."

Case Analysis #13: Title IX
Men can be barred from a women's volleyball team even if there is
no team for men as long as men's overall athletic opportunities
have not been limited relative to women's and if the school otherwise has met its obligations to effectively accomodate the interests
and abilities of both sexes.

159

LAW AWARENESS QUIZ

1. Must Not: Pregancy Discrimination Act prohibits different
   treatment of people because of pregnancy.

2. Must: Lau Guidelines and Title VI require all students with
   limited English proficiency be given instruction comparable to other students and a program to raise their
   proficiency.

3. May: Although First Amendment guarantees free speech and press,
   several states have laws requiring compensatory materials
   if texts are biased.

4. Must: P.L. 94-142 requires students thought to be handicapped
   go through evaluation process for certification; then
   IEP is done.

5. Must Not: Title IX prohibits different treatment of people
   because of sex.

6. Must: The Title IX self evaluation process requires administrators to make certain that students are not counseled
   differently.

7. Must Not: Title VI prohibits a school from requiring reading
   placement tests from minority students. The school
   could require all students to take a reading placement test.

8. May: In contact sports, under Title IX, a school may either
   sponsor separate teams for both sexes or allow both sexes
   to try out for one team.

9. Must Not: Title IX prohibits different treatment because of sex.

10. Must: First Amendment freedom of religion

11. Must Not: Pregnancy Discrimination Act prohibits different treat-
    of people because of prenancy.

12. Must Not: Students may be segregated for contact sports, but
    must be allowed to enroll in any class.

MY AWARENESS AND UNDERSTANDING OF CHILD ABUSE AND NEGLECT
True/False :

1. False : Neglect is reported approximately twice as often as abuse. (Data... 1980, p.1)

2. True : Even with all the problems of "counting systems" and reporting the data is becoming more consistent. Although a uniform method is still in the process of being developed. Currently, the problem lies in interpretation and state-to state laws.

3. True : Hare, "Reflections...," 1980, p.4.

4. True : Swartz, Mimi, " The Pass-Along Problem." Houston p. 247.

5. True : It would be worthy to check your particular state law(s) regarding your role as a classroom teacher in reporting/suspecting child abuse or neglect.(Stein,81)

6. True : Ellerstein, 1981, p.1

7. False : Stein, 1981.

Multiple Choice:

1. 84-97% : Stein, 1981 p. 63; Hare, "Réflections.." p.2.

2. 1-3% : Ellerstein, 1981, p.4

3. 50% : Woldenstein, 1976, p.310.

4. 20-10% : Conte, 1980.

5. 80% : Canavan, 1981.(Edited by Ellerstein)

6. 12% : Hare, p.8